HEALTHCARE CAREER STARTER

by Cheryl Hancock

Copyright © 1998 Learning Express, LLC.

All rights reserved under International and Pan-American Copyright Conventions. Published in the United States by LearningExpress, LLC, New York.

Library of Congress Cataloging-in-Publication Data

Hancock, Cheryl.
    Healthcare career starter/Cheryl Hancock.
        p.   cm.
    Includes bibliographical references (p.).
    ISBN   1–57685–095–1
    1. Allied health personnel—Vocational guidance.
I. Title.
R697.A4H34   1998
610.69—dc21   98–4827
                                                                   CIP

Printed in the United States of America
9 8 7 6 5 4 3 2 1
First Edition

Regarding the Information in this Book
Every effort has been made to ensure accuracy of directory information up until press time. However, phone numbers and/or addresses are subject to change. Please contact the respective organization for the most recent information.

For Further Information
For information on LearningExpress, other LearningExpress products, or bulk sales, please call or write to us at:
    LearningExpress™
    900 Broadway
    Suite 604
    New York, NY 10003
    212-995-2566

LearningExpress is an affiliated company of Random House, Inc.

ISBN 1-57685-095-1

CONTENTS

Introduction	Why Enter the Healthcare Field?	v
Chapter One	The Hottest Healthcare Jobs and How to Get Them	1
Chapter Two	All About Training Programs	25
Chapter Three	Directory of Healthcare Training Programs	43
Chapter Four	Financial Aid for the Training You Need	89
Chapter Five	How to Land Your First Job	105
Chapter Six	How to Succeed Once You've Landed the Job	129
Appendix A	List of Professional Associations	141
Appendix B	Additional Resources	149

ABOUT THE AUTHOR

Cheryl Hancock is a freelance writer and editor based in Athens, Georgia, as well as a wife and a mother of two. She is also the author of a book entitled *EMT Career Starter*.

INTRODUCTION

WHY ENTER THE HEALTHCARE FIELD?

The healthcare industry is growing at an enormous rate, creating a wealth of entry-level positions. Currently, approximately nine million individuals are employed as healthcare workers, and the healthcare industry is expected to produce approximately four million more jobs by the year 2005. This is almost double the rate of growth of all other (non-farm) wage and salary employment.

There are many ways to break into the healthcare field. This book tells you about the hottest entry-level positions and how you can land great jobs in these areas. High entry-level pay and rapid pay increases make employment in the healthcare field quite inviting. Most entry-level positions begin at or near the $15,000 (nursing aide) to $30,000 (surgical tech) a year range, with training programs ranging from three months to two years. You can obtain any of the jobs discussed in this book without getting a four-year college degree, and some require as little as a three-month certificate program. The healthcare field offers a wide range of choices; this book gives you the information you need to select the healthcare career and training program that are right for you.

In chapter one you'll get an inside look at the hottest healthcare jobs, specific job descriptions, typical salaries, advancement opportunities, hiring trends, and the skills needed for each job. Then there's a step-by-step checklist for entering and succeeding in the healthcare field. You'll find out the difference between working in a hospital setting and an outpatient center and learn about other types of employers and their typical hiring procedures.

Chapter two tells you why you need formal training and how to select and evaluate training programs near you. You'll find sample courses that are taught in actual training programs for each of the hottest entry-level job titles in this book. These course descriptions can help you decide what occupation is right for you and how long you need to go to school for each one. When you talk to admissions counselors in training programs you're considering, you can use the checklist in chapter two to ask tough questions that will help you evaluate the quality of the program. Sample course descriptions show you what to look for in each training program. There also are tips on how to get the most out of your training program, such as how to study for exams, take notes in class, and network with other students.

The directory of healthcare training programs in chapter three includes a representative listing of schools by city, state, and job title so you can look up the training programs in your area. If you're considering moving to a new city, you can check that city's programs too. All school listings include name, address, and phone number so you can contact each school directly to get more information and application forms.

After you've selected a training program that's right for you, chapter four explains how financial aid can help you pay for it. A step-by-step look at the financial aid process will prepare you to apply for and receive aid as soon as possible.

Chapter five shows you how to land the job you want after you complete your training program. You'll find hot tips on where to look for openings and the latest information on networking, writing resumes and cover letters, and using the World Wide Web to find your dream job. Samples resumes from healthcare workers are included. Finally, chapter six shows you how to succeed once you've landed your job.

So read on to find out how you can enter and succeed in the exciting and growing healthcare field.

CHAPTER 1

> This chapter describes the hottest entry-level healthcare jobs you can get with two years of training or less, so you can begin your career in healthcare as soon as possible. It includes specific job descriptions, typical salaries, advancement opportunities, hiring trends, and the skills needed for each job. You'll learn about different types of employers and their typical hiring procedures, including alternatives to hospital work. You'll also find inside advice from healthcare workers.

THE HOTTEST HEALTHCARE JOBS AND HOW TO GET THEM

This book focuses on the following entry-level positions with high growth potential: dental assistant, medical assistant, nursing assistant, physical therapist assistant, radiologic technician, and surgical technician. The wealth of jobs available make all of these positions a possibility for your future. A nursing recruiter from the town of Highland, New York, has this encouraging comment for people considering entering one of these fields:

> Anyone entering the healthcare field in any area is almost guaranteed an entry-level position wherever they intend to establish their career. At our hospital, we hired 500 key entry-level people for positions ranging from nursing aides to clerical

assistants last year alone, mostly because of the progression of entry-level people into higher positions.

Some people want to enter the healthcare field in one area and then seek additional training for more advanced positions, and others are happy to stay in the position they started in. The healthcare field offers you the flexibility to make such decisions because both alternatives are within reach. A heart surgeon from Atlanta, Georgia, tells how he got his start in the healthcare field:

> Healthcare seemed like the most logical choice for my future since I like working with people. I wanted a helping profession, one that gave me the satisfaction of helping my fellow human. I began as a surgical technologist with a hospital and really enjoyed my work. After a while, I decided I wanted to be a surgeon, so I went back to school part time and then full time after receiving extra student loans. I eventually became an intern, then a practicing emergency physician. That's when I discovered my interest in heart surgery. I found my niche after a while, and I pursued it. Now I am head of the cardiovascular surgery department.

On the other hand, you might want to stay in the career you initially choose. A surgical technician explains:

> I have always been fascinated with surgery and what goes on in the operating room. The human body is so delicate and intricate. Each organ and muscle and nerve has its own function. I was never the type to be scared of blood or of watching someone being cut open, but I never wanted to be the one cutting. I enjoy knowing the secrets to the inside of the body without actually having the responsibility of fixing it. I thought about being a doctor when I was little, but now being a surgical technician is what I always want to be.

Read on for the inside information you need to pursue one of the hot areas in the healthcare field.

DENTAL ASSISTANTS
Description of Typical Duties

Dental assistants perform a variety of patient care, administrative, and laboratory duties, including the tasks listed below. Of course, not all dental assistants do all of these things; duties depend on the needs of each dental office.

- Dental assistants may work chairside as dentists examine and treat patients, or they may have administrative duties such as scheduling appointments, receiving patients, keeping treatment records, sending bills, receiving payments, and ordering supplies.
- They make patients as comfortable as possible in the dental chair, prepare them for treatment, and obtain dental records.
- They hand instruments and materials to dentists and keep the patient's mouth dry and clear by using suction or other devices.
- Assistants also sterilize and disinfect instruments and equipment, prepare tray setups for dental procedures, provide postoperative instruction, and instruct patients in oral healthcare.
- Some dental assistants prepare materials for making impressions and restoration, expose radiographs, and process dental x-ray film as directed by a dentist.
- They may also remove sutures, apply anesthetics and cavity preventive agents to teeth and gums, remove cement used in the filling process, and place rubber dams on the teeth to isolate them for individual treatment.
- Assistants with laboratory duties make casts of teeth and mouth from impressions taken by dentists and make temporary crowns.

Aimee Davidson, a dental assistant from North Carolina describes her job:

> My job is very demanding. Besides being a chairside assistant, I also order all the supplies for the office, deal with all the vendors, handle all the lab cases coming in and out of the office, and help the receptionists when they need it. When the dentist doesn't need me, I write up lab slips, stock rooms, check my supplies, and keep a running list of what needs to be done that day. I never have time to stand around. There is always something to be done.

Typical Salaries

On average, dental assistants earn $18,000 to $27,000 or more annually working full time, depending on the amount of training they have received. When they gain more experience, they earn higher salaries.

Hiring Trends

Employment for dental assistants is expected to grow 70 percent through the year 2005. Most job openings for dental assistants are with group or private practices; some work in dental schools and government hospitals. Job openings arise when assistants leave the occupation or decide to further their education.

Personal Abilities and Personality Traits Needed

Dentists look for assistants who are reliable and who have good people skills and manual dexterity. Dental assistants need to be able to handle instruments carefully and quickly. Their work area is usually beside the dentist's chair, so they become the dentist's extra hand.

Advancement Opportunities

With additional training, a dental assistant can move up to become a level II dental assistant or a dental hygienist, performing limited work on patients under the supervision of a dentist. Without further education, advancement opportunities are limited. Some dental assistants working the front office become office managers. Others, working chairside, go back to school to become dental hygienists.

MEDICAL ASSISTANTS
Description of Typical Duties

Medical assistants perform routine clinical and clerical tasks to keep hospitals and the offices of physicians, podiatrists, chiropractors, dentists, optometrists, and other healthcare professionals running smoothly. Clinical and clerical duties vary from office to office depending on the office's size, location, and specialty.

- Medical assistants may be restricted to typical office duties at a hospital but may have clinical duties at a small clinic.
- They answer telephones, greet patients, update and file patient medical records, fill out insurance forms, schedule appointments, arrange for

hospital admission and laboratory services, and handle billing and bookkeeping.
- Medical assistants' clinical duties vary according to state law; they may include taking medical histories and recording vital signs, explaining treatment procedures to patients, preparing patients for examination, and assisting during routine examinations.
- Medical assistants also collect and prepare laboratory specimens, perform basic lab tests, dispose of contaminated supplies, and sterilize medical instruments.
- They instruct patients about medication and special diets, prepare and administer medications, authorize drug refills, telephone prescriptions to a pharmacy, draw blood, prepare patients for x-rays, remove sutures, and change dressings.

Typical Salaries

On average, a medical assistant earns $18,000 to $21,000 or more annually. Wages for medical assistants with less than two years of experience range from $8 to $11 an hour; those with five years of experience earn $10 to $14 an hour.

Hiring Trends

Medical assistant jobs are projected to increase 71 percent or more by the year 2005. Most medical assistant positions are in the offices of physicians and other health practitioners such as chiropractors, optometrists, and podiatrists. Others work in hospitals, nursing homes, and other healthcare facilities. Employment growth will be driven by the growth in the number of group practices, clinics, and other healthcare facilities that need a large support staff—particularly the flexible medical assistant, who can handle both clinical and clerical duties.

Personal Abilities and Personality Traits Needed

Like all healthcare workers, medical assistants must have the desire to help people. Medical assistants deal with the public, so they must be neat and well groomed and have a courteous, pleasant manner. They must be able to put patients at ease, explain physicians' instructions, and respect the confidential nature of medical information. A medical assistant's clinical duties require a reasonable level of manual dexterity as well as good eyesight.

Advancement Opportunities

Medical assistants can move up to office management, administration, personnel management, or human resources management positions. They may qualify for a wide variety of administrative support jobs, and they can teach medical assisting. Some, with additional training, enter health occupations such as nursing or medical technology.

NURSING ASSISTANTS

Description of Typical Duties

Nursing assistants, also known as nursing aides or hospital attendants, work under the supervision of nursing and medical staff.

- They answer patients' call bells, deliver messages, serve meals and help patients eat, make beds, and dress and bathe patients.
- Nursing assistants may also take care of patients' skin and take their temperature, pulse, respiration, and blood pressure.
- They may also escort patients to operating and examining rooms, set up equipment, or store and move supplies.
- They may have to move patients in and out of bed or help them stand or walk.

Nursing aides and home-healthcare aides share similar jobs, but the home-healthcare aide works at the patient's home. Nursing aides employed in nursing homes often are the principal caregivers and have far more contact with residents than do other members of the staff.

Typical Salaries

On average, nursing aides earn $13,000 to $15,000 annually. Assistants, who have a certificate, earn $15,000 to $16,000 or more annually.

Hiring Trends

Employment for nursing aides and assistants is projected to increase 50 percent by the year 2005. About half of all nursing aides work in nursing homes, and about one-quarter work in hospitals. Modern medical technology, nursing and personal care facilities, and the expansion of nursing homes and long-term care facilities will increase the employment of nursing aides and assistants.

Personal Abilities and Personality Traits Needed

Nursing aides and other assistants who work directly with sick or injured patients should be tactful, patient, understanding, emotionally stable, and dependable, and, as stated previously, they should have a desire to help people. Assistants also should be able to work as part of a team and be willing to perform repetitive, routine tasks. Joseph Bandspiegel, Ph.D., from Roseland Surgical Center, Roseland, New Jersey, explains that the healthcare worker's task isn't always easy:

> All healthcare workers must be calm by nature yet aggressive in order to perform their various activities effectively. They must know how to deal with the public and must be "nice" at all times. This won't always be easy, because those under duress aren't always the easiest to work with. However, healthcare workers cannot put a patient under more stress by showing a poor attitude.

Advancement Opportunities

For aides, opportunities for advancement are limited. To enter other health occupations, aides generally need additional formal training. Some employers and unions provide opportunities by simplifying the educational paths to advancement. Experience as an aide can also help you decide whether to pursue additional training for another career in the healthcare field. A registered nurse from Cleveland, Ohio, explains:

> When I was being interviewed for nursing school, the admissions committee asked me what I hoped to be doing in five or ten years. I really didn't know what I wanted to do years into the future, because my only thought was getting into the nursing program. I thought I should sound ambitious, so I said that I would like to be in an administrative position by then. I was accepted into the program, so that must have been what they wanted to hear. I began as a nursing assistant, and with a couple more years of training, I eventually became a registered nurse. I found the whole experience extremely rewarding, and I thought I might like to move up into administration as I'd said in my interview. However, I found that moving away from patients and co-worker camaraderie wasn't

what I wanted to do. I am happy I became a registered nurse, and I am happy to stay here.

PHYSICAL THERAPY ASSISTANTS
Description of Typical Duties
Physical therapy assistants, also known as physical therapy aides, prepare patients both physically and psychologically for therapy and instruct patients in a wide variety of treatments.

- Assistants may aid patients who need to exercise on a treadmill or stationary bike or in a swimming pool or use weight-lifting equipment.
- Assistants help administer massages, electrical stimulation, paraffin baths, hot/cold packs, and traction.
- Assistants may measure a patient's size, flexibility, and range of motion or use ultrasound equipment to evaluate patients' discomfort in a knee, elbow, or other joint.
- Most importantly, physical therapy assistants encourage patients during therapy sessions and make sure they perform exercises correctly to achieve maximum benefit and avoid further injury.

Typical Salaries
On average, a licensed physical therapy assistant earns $26,000 to $40,000 or more annually, depending on years of experience. A nonlicensed physical therapy aide makes $16,000 to $26,000 annually.

Hiring Trends
Physical therapist assistant jobs are expected to increase by 93 percent or more by the year 2005. A shortage of physical therapists in many areas makes licensed assistants an attractive alternative. Over half of all assistants and aides work in hospitals or private physical therapy offices. Others work in clinics, nursing homes, and even inside patients' homes. In sports medicine, they may work part time on the sidelines or in swimming pools performing aqua therapy.

Personal Abilities and Personality Traits Needed
For a physical therapy assistant or aide, personal requirements differ vastly from those of many other healthcare jobs. These assistants need a moderate amount of

physical strength and stamina to assist patients with treatment. Constant kneeling, stooping, and standing are all part of the job. In some cases, assistants may need to help lift patients, so those prone to back problems are strongly advised not to become physical therapy assistants.

Advancement Opportunities

With specific training, physical therapist aides advance to licensed physical therapist assistants; with more training, they eventually can become physical therapists. Licensed physical therapist assistants can administer many more aspects of the treatment prescribed by the therapist than can unlicensed aides.

RADIOLOGIC TECHNOLOGISTS

Description of Typical Duties

There are three different types of radiologic technologists: radiographers, radiation therapy technologists, and sonographers.

Radiographers

- Radiographers produce x-ray films of parts of the human body for use in diagnosing medical problems.
- They prepare patients for radiologic exams by explaining the procedure, removing any jewelry, and positioning patients so the correct body part can be radiographed.
- They place the x-ray film under the part of the patient's body to be examined and make the exposure. They then remove the film and develop it.

Radiation Therapy Technologists

- Radiation therapy technologists prepare cancer patients for treatment and administer prescribed doses of ionizing radiation to specific body parts.
- They position patients under high-energy linear accelerators to expose affected body parts to treatment.
- They check the patient for radiation side effects such as nausea, hair loss, and skin irritation.
- They give instructions and explanations to patients who are likely to be very ill.

Sonographers

- Sonographers, also known as ultrasound technologists, use machines that project high-frequency sound waves into areas of the patient's body that reflect echoes and form an image.
- They explain the procedure, record additional medical history, and position the patient for testing.
- They look for subtle differences between healthy and pathological areas.

Typical Salaries

Radiologic technologists earn, on average, $28,000 to $42,000, depending on their education level and length of training.

Hiring Trends

Employment of radiologic technologists is expected to grow 70 percent through the year 2005. Current and new uses of imaging equipment will increase demand. Radiologic technologists are chiefly employed by hospitals.

Personal Abilities and Personality Traits Needed

Technologists are on their feet for long periods and may lift or turn disabled patients frequently. They work at machines but may also do some procedures at patients' bedsides. They must follow precise physician instructions and regulations concerning use of radiation to ensure that they, patients, and coworkers are protected from overexposure.

Radiation therapists, in contrast to other radiologic technologists, must be patient and sensitive. They may be prone to emotional "burnout" because they regularly treat extremely ill and dying patients.

Advancement Opportunities

With experience and additional training, staff technologists may become specialists and may be promoted to supervisor, chief radiologic technologist, or department administrator or director. Some technologists progress by becoming instructors or directors in radiologic technology programs; others take jobs as sales representatives or instructors with equipment manufacturers.

Radiation therapy technologists can specialize as medical radiation dosimetrists. Dosimetrists work with health physicists and oncologists (physicians who specialize in the study and treatment of tumors) to develop treatment plans.

Sonographers advance by specializing in a particular area: neurosurgery (the brain), vascular (blood flow), echocardiography (the heart), abdominal (the liver, kidneys, spleen, and pancreas), obstetrics/gynecology (the female reproductive system), or ophthalmology (the eye).

Jean Davis, a radiological technologist from Louisville, Kentucky shares her success story:

> I never realized how many positions would be open for a rad tech when I graduated from my training courses. I am not really good at dealing with patients, which I figured out when I first became a nurse assistant. I became friends with a radiologic technologist at the hospital I worked in, and that's when I decided to make a job change. I hadn't invested too much in being a nurse assistant, so I switched careers. I was very interested in taking x-rays and developing them, but I was especially interested in working with machines instead of patients. The x-rays seemed so hard to read, which was a great challenge. Now I feel like an expert when medical faculty have to come to me for explanations of x-rays. I am very happy in my job.

SURGICAL TECHNOLOGISTS
Description of Typical Duties

Surgical technologists, also called surgical or operating room technicians, assist in operations under the supervision of surgeons, registered nurses, or other surgical personnel.

- Before an operation, surgical technologists help set up the operating room with surgical instruments and equipment, sterile linens, and sterile solutions.
- They assemble, adjust, and check nonsterile equipment to ensure that it is working properly.
- Surgical technologists also prepare patients for surgery by washing, shaving, and disinfecting incision sites on patients.
- They transport patients to the operating room, help position them on the operating table, and cover them with sterile surgical drapes.
- They also observe patients' vital signs, check charts, and help the surgical team scrub and put on gloves, gowns, and masks.

Typical Salaries

Surgical technologists, on average, earn between $28,000 and $40,000, depending on their training and experience.

Hiring Trends

As the volume of surgery increases and operating room staffing patterns change, employment for surgical technologists is expected to increase 71 percent by the year 2005. Most surgical technologists are employed by hospitals, mainly in operating and delivery rooms. Some, called private scrubs, are employed directly by surgeons who have special surgical teams. Technological advances will require more surgical procedures, and the movement to outpatient or ambulatory surgery will mean rapid growth for surgical technologists in physicians' offices and clinics, including surgical centers.

Personal Abilities and Personality Traits Needed

Surgical technologists work in clean, well-lighted, and cool environments, and they must stand for long periods of time. At times they may be exposed to communicable diseases and unpleasant sights, odors, and materials. Surgical technologists need manual dexterity to handle instruments quickly. They also must be conscientious, orderly, and emotionally stable to handle the demands of the operating room environment. Surgical technologists must respond quickly and know procedures well, so they can get instruments ready for surgeons without having to be told.

Advancement Opportunities

Surgical technologists advance by specializing in a particular area of surgery, such as neurosurgery or open heart surgery. They may also work as circulating technologists or *nonsterile* members of surgical teams, preparing patients, helping with anesthesia, obtaining, opening, and holding packages for the *sterile* workers during procedures, interviewing patients before surgery, and so on. With additional training, some technologists advance to first assistants, who help with retracting, sponging, suturing, cauterizing bleeders, and closing and treating wounds; others become registered nurses. Mike Melillo, Jr., a surgical technologist from Roseland Surgical Center in New Jersey, notes:

This position is unique in that if you're good and you make an impression on the right people, it can lead you to work for a doctor privately, which is about as high as you can get without school. Obtaining more schooling will put you one step ahead of having the required experience for the operating room. You would also make a very good OR (operating room) nurse.

HOW TO BECOME A HEALTHCARE WORKER

The healthcare field is an explosive arena for job growth. Entry-level jobs such as dental assistants, medical assistants, nursing assistants, physical therapy assistants, surgical technologists, and radiologic technologists are the positions many hospitals and other doctors' practices are continually seeking to fill. You can enter and succeed in these occupations by following these steps:

- Graduate from high school or obtain a GED.
- Conduct a self-evaluation.
- Decide on an area of specialization.
- Find a training program that suits your needs.
- Complete the training program.
- Conduct your job search.
- Succeed in your first job.

In almost every city, the local public school system offers youth apprenticeships that guide high school students into the healthcare field with firsthand experience and a certificate that helps them get a job or enter a training program immediately after graduation.

However, if you are not in a high school or apprenticeship program, the first step to becoming a healthcare worker is to graduate from high school or get an equivalency degree (GED), which you can do through most adult education centers in your area.

Since there are many areas of specialization in the healthcare field, you need to decide where you might fit in best. Writing a self-profile will help you evaluate your abilities and personality traits.

Evaluating Yourself

Julie Jacobs, a medical assistant from Atlanta, Georgia, explains the strengths she discovered in herself, which she used to promote herself in the workplace:

> I'm a great talker, and I've experienced a lot of things. I find it easy to talk to just about anyone, especially nervous and uptight patients who would rather be anywhere but the waiting room of a doctor's office. I am also very self-motivated and well organized. I care about people and like being able to help them. I am very dedicated to what I love, and I'm hard-working. I loved science and related courses in school, so a career in healthcare seemed only natural.

Your self-evaluation will help show you a path to take. Your strengths and weaknesses can guide you, so take this step seriously.

Begin your evaluation by deciding how much training you wish to pursue and commit to. For example, a certificate can take three to six months to a year, an associate degree requires two years of training, and a bachelor's degree takes four years. (See chapter two for detailed information on all these types of programs.) Also, think about your areas of interest and what you do well. What skills do you most enjoy using? Write down your skills, gifts, and talents, and then prioritize them in order of importance.

List all the jobs you've ever had, including summer jobs, volunteer work, part-time jobs, and any freelance or short-term assignments you've done. Then add a similar list of your hobbies and other activities, including any special experiences you've had, such as babysitting or travel.

Do the same for your education, listing the school(s) you attended, your major courses of study, grades, special awards or honors, courses you particularly enjoyed, and extracurricular activities. These lists may begin to show you a likely career pattern.

Work environment is another key consideration in choosing a healthcare career. Some people are happiest in a setting with lots of other people and activity. The hospital environment would be perfect for them. Others feel more comfortable in a well-defined, secluded, intimate, personalized environment. They might prefer a laboratory, a cubicle, or a quiet room to work in.

An experienced counselor can be of great help in the decision-making process. Counselors can give you a series of vocational interest and aptitude tests, and they can interpret and explain the results. Vocational testing and counseling are offered in guidance departments of high schools, vocational schools, and colleges. Some local offices of the state employment services affiliated with the federal employment service offer free counseling. Counselors will not tell you what to do, but they can help guide you in your search for a specialization.

Evaluating yourself will help tell you what type of job you'll be good at performing. You also may find it helpful to create a checklist such as the following:

- Do you want to work with patients or machines?
- Do you prefer to work on a team or individually?
- Do you want good benefits or a chance for quick promotion?
- Do you want a variety of tasks or a few routine duties?
- What is your physical stamina or strength?

These questions can help you choose the job that best fits your particular circumstances and needs. Compare your answers with the descriptions of jobs listed earlier in this chapter to find a match.

TYPES OF EMPLOYERS

For each healthcare position discussed in this book, there are many different types of employers. The most general employer is a *hospital,* offering a multitude of positions for entry-level job seekers. Hospitals are described as short-stay or long-term, depending on how much time a patient spends there before being discharged. The most common type of hospital is the *community* or *general hospital,* typically a small hospital where most people receive care.

A *teaching hospital* provides clinical training for medical students and other medical professionals and is usually part of a major medical school. *Public hospitals* are owned and operated by federal, state, or city governments, are usually located in the inner cities, and often treat patients who are unable to pay for services or who depend on Medicaid payments.

In *group medical practices,* which are very common, two or more doctors share a building or office, and each doctor may have a separate staff. The doctors share the expenses of the building. These practices may include optometrists, chiropractors, dentists, or other professionals and can range from large organizations to small offices with one or two assistants.

Health maintenance organizations (HMOs) are group practices organized to provide complete coverage for subscribers' health needs at a pre-established price. The patients (or their employers) pay a set amount each month; in turn, the HMO group provides care such as routine checkups at no extra charge, or at a very minimal charge. Members are usually locked into the plan for a specified period of time—usually one year—and if the service they need is available within the HMO, they must use a selected HMO doctor.

Mental health facilities provide medication, emotional support, and physical support to mentally ill patients.

Hospices provide support and care for terminally ill people in the final stage of their disease so they can live as comfortably and fully as possible. A hospice offers a program of services for both patients and their families so they can make the necessary preparations for death. A hospice may be a freestanding institution, a special wing at a hospital, or simply a few beds that can be made available to the program as needed.

Home healthcare provides nursing services in patients' homes. Patients may be any age and include those who expect to get better and resume work and daily activities as well as those who expect to die. Care may include everything from giving medication to providing physical therapy to housekeeping.

Nursing homes provide long-term care for elderly patients. There are three types of nursing homes. A *residential care facility (RCF)* normally provides meals and housekeeping for the resident, plus some basic medical monitoring, and is geared toward residents who are fairly independent and do not need constant medical attention.

An *intermediate care facility (ICF)* offers room and board and nursing care as necessary for those who can no longer live independently. A s*killed nursing facility (SNF)* provides round-the-clock nursing care plus physician coverage and is for patients who need intensive care plus services such as occupational therapy, physical therapy, and rehabilitation. Each of these facilities provides exercise and social programs as well.

Surgicenters, also called outpatient centers, are ambulatory surgery centers equipped to perform routine surgical procedures that do not require an overnight stay. A surgicenter does not need the sophisticated and expensive equipment found in a hospital operating room. Minor surgery, such as abortions, tissue biopsies, hernia repair, cataract surgery, and some forms of cosmetic surgery are typically performed in these facilities.

Emergency clinics or *urgicenters* are usually run by private for-profit organizations and provide up to 24-hour care on a drop-in basis. They offer quick help in an emergency when the nearest hospital is miles away, and they usually are open during the hours that most doctor's offices are closed. To minimize costs, they do not provide hospital beds. They deal with problems such as cuts that require sutures, sprains and bruises from accidents, and various infections.

Surgical technologist Michael Melillo, Jr., from Roseland Surgical Center in New Jersey, contrasts working at a surgical center and at a hospital:

> The differences between the center I work at and most hospitals are smaller staff, fewer cases, and no really sick people. In the hospital most people who come in are at death's door, sometimes not even able to decide what is going to happen to them because they are so sick. But at the center, the work is done electively, so the patients, for the most part, are healthy and aware of what is happening to them before surgery.

HEALTHCARE JOB DESCRIPTIONS

The following job descriptions will give you an idea of what's involved in many healthcare fields. You can become an aide or an assistant in any of these specialty positions. Instead of a physical therapist assistant, you could become an art therapist assistant if arts and sciences are your strengths, or you could work as an assistant in the private practice of a dance therapist. You could become a medical assistant employed by an audiologist, a genetics counselor, or a chiropractor. You could become a surgical technologist in a hospital or for an emergency clinic. Ronald Shane, an optometrist from Pennsylvania, describes his practice:

> I am in a solo professional practice with no in-house optical lab. Usually the only additional help I have is a receptionist who is also the bookkeeper, secretary, and jack of all trades. In a larger, busier practice you would find additional help, such as an optometric assistant and perhaps a dispensing optician, as well as other personnel such as contact lens trainers. Many skill levels are required for medical practices.

- **Art therapists** are trained in the fine arts and the behavioral sciences to develop rehabilitation programs that use art materials and techniques (such as painting, sculpting with clay, making crafts).
- **Audiologists** test, diagnose, and treat people who have hearing and related problems.

- **Biochemists** study and research the chemical composition of living things, focusing on processes such as metabolism, reproduction, growth, and heredity.
- **Biomedical engineers** use engineering skills and concepts to invent or improve devices, instruments, and substances used in treating medical problems (for example, pacemakers, ultrasound equipment, and artificial limbs).
- **Blood bank technologists** are medical technologists who specialize in the skills and knowledge needed to maintain a blood bank, such as drawing, classifying, testing, analyzing, and storing blood.
- **Cardiopulmonary technologists** conduct tests and evaluations related to the diagnosis and treatment of heart (cardiac) and lung (pulmonary) diseases and disorders.
- **Cardiovascular technicians** assist physicians and other medical personnel in diagnosing and treating medical problems related to the body's heart (cardiac) and blood vessel (peripheral vascular) systems.
- **Chiropractors** diagnose and treat medical problems related to the body's muscular, nervous, and skeletal systems, especially the spine.
- **Dance therapists** are trained in dance/movement, psychology, and physiology to treat and rehabilitate patients with emotional or physical disorders, or developmental disabilities.
- **Dental hygienists** perform preventive dental procedures, including cleaning teeth, and instruct patients on oral hygiene practices to prevent teeth and gum abnormalities or disease.
- **Dentists** diagnose, prevent, and treat problems of the teeth and tissues of the mouth.
- **Dietitians** plan nutrition programs and supervise meal preparation and service, often for large institutions such as hospitals, schools, nursing homes, and prisons.
- **EEG technologists** conduct tests using EEG (electroencephalograph) equipment, which records electrical impulses in the brain, to assist neurologists (physicians who study the brain) in treating patients with neural disorders such as brain tumors, strokes, and Alzheimer's disease.
- **EKG technicians** are cardiovascular technicians who perform EKG (electrocardiogram) testing to record and monitor electrical impulses transmitted by the heart.

- **Genetic counselors** advise patients, often prospective parents, on matters related to hereditary diseases and disorders such as Down's Syndrome, muscular dystrophy, and prebirth spinal or organ malformations.
- **Licensed practical nurses** provide basic nursing care (both medical and nonmedical) to sick, injured, convalescing, and handicapped patients under the direction of physicians and registered nurses.
- **Medical illustrators** use artistic skills and medical and anatomical knowledge to create drawings, diagrams, models, and other graphic aids for use in medical research, publications, consultations, exhibits, teaching, and various communications media.
- **Optometrists** diagnose and treat vision problems, prescribing and fitting eyeglasses and contact lenses, and may provide basic care for eye disorders such as cataracts and glaucoma (unlike ophthalmologists, however, who are physicians specializing in the treatment of eye diseases and injuries).
- **Orthotists** design, build, and fit devices to support weak body parts or correct physical defects, such as limb or spinal cord disorders stemming from cerebral palsy, polio, or stroke.
- **Pharmacists** dispense drugs prescribed by physicians and other medical practitioners, advise patients about medications, and consult with physicians about the selection, dosages, and effects of medications.
- **Physical therapists** rehabilitate people who suffer from physical disabilities caused by accidents or disease, using massage, water instruction, machine movement, or other methods.
- **Podiatrists** are doctors who diagnose and treat disorders, diseases, and injuries of the foot and lower leg.
- **Prosthetists** design, build, and fit artificial limbs (prostheses) for patients who have lost part or all of their own limbs due to accident, illness, or a congenital condition.
- **Psychologists** study human behavior and mental processes to understand, explain, and change people's behavior, often within an area of specialty such as clinical, developmental, organizational, or research psychology.
- **Recreation therapists** use games, sports, exercises, arts and crafts, and other recreational activities to treat patients with emotional, physical, or mental disorders and help them develop effective social and interpersonal skills.

- **Registered nurses** provide direct and indirect patient care, including assessing, planning, implementing, and evaluating care in areas ranging from pediatrics to geriatrics.
- **Respiratory therapists** evaluate, treat, and care for patients with breathing disorders such as asthma and emphysema and provide emergency care for heart failure, stroke, drowning, or shock victims.
- **Surgeons** work in the operating rooms of hospitals performing surgery on patients. Many surgeons specialize in a particular area of the body.

TYPICAL HIRING PROCEDURES

Among most hospitals and physicians' centers, the hiring procedures are similar. Applicants normally fill out an application for employment and participate in an interview. Many employers prefer that applicants fill out the application on site, so remember to bring all necessary information you may not readily recall. You should also bring along several copies of your resume, and submit one with your application. The human resources representative or employment recruiter may talk briefly with you when you turn in your application. Bringing everything with you will impress the employment recruiter.

For most positions, the employer will request that you take a drug test and a physical. They usually will conduct a criminal background check and screen your references.

At certain hospitals and other institutions, you cannot apply for a position unless it is posted on the job board or if applications have been requested. You may be offered a job description that will outline the duties and experience required for the position. Job titles may vary at different institutions, but the duties involved will be similar. On the next page is a sample job posting for a medical assistant at a hospital.

Job openings are posted at hospitals for about five days, on average, and may be updated weekly. Many hospitals offer a job hotline number so prospective employees can keep up with the job openings. Smaller practices may take out ads in the newspapers or consult local hospitals for applicants.

The Application

If you have ever filled out an application for any kind of job, school, or financial aid before, the application for an entry-level position in healthcare will be similar. The application will ask for the following information:

The Hottest Healthcare Jobs and How to Get Them

> **Title: Medical Assistant (or Patient Care Technician)**
>
> **Job Summary:** Provides direct patient care under the direction of a registered nurse or licensed practical nurse according to policy and procedure. Contributes to the safe and effective operation of the nursing unit. Provides direct patient care primarily for patients ages 12 and up.
>
> **Education:** High school diploma or equivalent
>
> **Licensure:** None
>
> **Experience:** Previous exposure to training
>
> **Skills:** Skills basic to completion of medical assistant course
>
> **Essential Physical and Mental Functions and Environmental Conditions:** Able to see objects closely, as in reading, frequently. Able to see objects far away frequently. Able to discriminate color and perceive depth frequently.
>
> Able to hear normal sounds with some background noise, as in answering telephone, frequently. Able to distinguish sounds, as in voice patterns, frequently.
>
> Able to give and receive verbal communications continuously. Able to read and write written communications continuously.
>
> Able to carry objects weighing 10 pounds or more frequently; able to carry objects weighing 49 pounds or less on occasion.
>
> Able to sit 30 minutes consecutively, 1 hour per shift. Able to stand in place 10 minutes consecutively, 1 hour per shift. Able to remain on feet 4 hours consecutively, 7 hours per shift. Able to sustain awkward position 5 minutes consecutively, 2 hours per shift.
>
> Able to perform motor skills such as bending, twisting, turning, kneeling, reaching out, reaching up, wrist turning, grasping, finger manipulation, feeling perception, fast response, frequently.

- name, address, and social security number
- job information or previous work experience, including dates and reason for leaving
- skills or supervisory experience
- educational experience
- references, or you may be asked to sign a references release statement
- citizenship status

No question on the application should touch on a prospective employee's race, color, religion, national origin, age, sex, marital status, or disabilities. If there is such a question, you may leave it blank. The application should state that the company is an equal opportunity employer.

You will be asked to sign the application to verify that all the information is true and correct. The application will state that incorrect information is cause for immediate dismissal. Remember that the employer will verify the information, so it's best to be honest.

Your application will stay active on file at a hospital for six months. If you have not called to update it, it will be kept inactive for another six months. However, you may reapply or update your application at any time for other openings. In smaller healthcare practices, your application may or may not remain on file, depending on the size of the practice. Smaller practices usually do not have as high a turnover rate as hospitals, so there is little need to keep applications on file.

Employment Agencies

Employment agencies use the same hiring techniques as other companies. You will fill out an application, the agency will check your references, and, depending on the policy of the agency, you may have to take a drug test. The agency may or may not perform a criminal background check.

Employment agencies make money when you receive employment, so they want qualified candidates. A temporary agency recruiter from Washington, D.C., explains:

> Many people stay with temporary agencies because they can work at selected hours and on a part-time basis. Some women like the temporary field because they get the time they need for their children and still make some money. People can also work at different companies, sampling different environments to find a work environment that suits them. And there's a very realistic chance of finding permanent employment through temporary jobs.

Federal and State Hiring Procedures

Federal and state institutions must follow certain regulations when hiring employees. State regulations vary by state. These regulations are designed to make the hiring process fair for everyone. Although most hospitals hire according to federal and state hiring guidelines, many small practices do not. A chiropractor from Chicago, Illinois, explains:

> I don't think I use federal or state guidelines for hiring, except the most commonly known, such as not discriminating. I have a very small business, and only one medical assistant is required to keep my office running smoothly. When I plan to hire someone for the front, I place an ad in the newspaper and accept applications from people for about a week, depending on whether I need someone immediately or not. I usually decide based on the applicant's experience and knowledge of handling patients. I can tell through an interview and a resume whether the applicant is right for the job.

Federal and state hiring procedures help larger companies keep certain criteria in mind as they hire large numbers of people. Employment requirements are much stricter in federal and state owned and operated environments.

Examples of federal and state hiring procedures include:

- Companies must keep an application on active file for at least six months.
- Companies must clearly and adequately identify the requirements of a position in the vacancy announcement so that applicants understand the basis on which their application will be evaluated. This will also ensure that applicants possess the necessary skills to perform the work.
- Companies cannot set standards for any job that adversely affect the hiring chances of any one group of people, and the standards must be job-related, not person-related. *The Qualification Standards for General Schedule Positions,* or X-188, describes the legal standards of various jobs.
- Companies must interview at least three to five people for the opening.
- Companies cannot discriminate on the basis of race, religion, national origin, age, sex, marital status, or physical handicap.
- Any hiring tests must be related to the specific job for which the candidate has applied, and question responses cannot reduce the chances of minorities, women, or a disproportionate number of candidates in any single group.

THE INSIDE TRACK

Who:	Aimee Davidson
What:	Dental assistant I
Where:	Welborne & Welborne, D.D.S., Huntersville, North Carolina
How long:	14 months
How much:	$30,000 annual salary
Degree:	Three years of college
School:	University of Georgia, Central Piedmont Community College

Insider's Advice

When I was growing up, I always said I wanted to be a dentist. Somewhere around high school and my first year of college, I changed my mind. I think when you are that young, the thought of going to school for eight years seems so long. Now that I am 26, I have realized eight years is a very small amount of time in the whole grand scheme of things. I wish I had followed my dream right after high school, because I would be graduating from dental school right now.

My advice is to follow your dream straight through to the end. Decide what type of job would make you happy, and go for it with the realization that you want more from life. When I interviewed for my job, I was the only one out of ten who didn't have experience. Dr. Welborne later told me that he would have hired me on the spot if I had had some experience. However, the other applicants may have had the experience, but they didn't have the personality he wanted. As a dental assistant, you sit only about a foot away from the dentist for almost eight hours a day. I showed him how serious I was about my dreams and this job, and he gave me the chance I feel I deserved and still work hard for.

Insider's Take on the Future

My goal is to become a dentist. I am currently working on completing my bachelor's degree. I used to take classes at night and work full time, but now I work about 30 hours a week and take one or two classes a semester during the day. You don't have to have a four-year degree to be accepted into dental school. There are general requirements to meet and a Dental Admissions Test to take. A four-year degree improves your chances of getting in. I plan to take the DAT in the fall of 1998 and will submit my application for dental school with the hope of being accepted for the fall of 1999.

CHAPTER 2

ALL ABOUT TRAINING PROGRAMS

This chapter is all about the training you need for your future in healthcare. It explains why you need to get training and reviews the types of training courses that are available. Sample courses from training programs across the country will give you an idea of what types of programs and classes are offered for each job. You'll learn about work-study and internships and about choosing the right training program. There are tips on studying for exams, taking notes, networking with classmates, getting to know your instructor, and using the career placement or counseling office. You'll also find helpful interviews with employment recruiters, instructors, healthcare workers, and students who can give you the inside scoop.

Most jobs in the healthcare field, especially those jobs that involve direct patient treatment or operating equipment, require a period of training in a clinical setting so you can gain knowledge of hospital or physician office procedures. Requirements for entering the field often include the completion of a training program, such as obtaining some kind of certificate or associate degree. A hospital employment recruiter from Tampa, Florida, states:

> Most hospitals will not hire someone without state certified training. We do not train individuals who do not have any

experience because we have such a high volume of patients who need care. We need people who are familiar with their job and who meet the standards set by state or national certificate examinations. I would say 100 percent of the people we hire at our hospital have a certificate or degree of some kind, unless they are in a position such as housekeeping that does not require direct patient care.

Making Decisions About Training

Deciding on the right training program may seem challenging since there are so many choices. Remember the personal evaluation you created in chapter one? Use that evaluation to consider the questions below. Though you may not know the answers right away, this checklist can help you decide which training program is right for you and help you focus your career goals.

- Do I need a job now or can I wait and gain greater experience through education?
- How long do I want to be in school before getting a job?
- Am I interested in work-study or internships?
- What kind of financial aid can I receive from the school? Can I receive enough financial aid to attend a larger college or university?
- What school can I afford or be accepted to?
- How much will tuition, books, and tools cost?

Your budget and the cost of the training program will determine whether you should work part time and go to school part time, apply for financial aid, or participate in work-study, and whether you can afford an institute, a college, or a university.

- What schools are in my area?
- Can I or do I want to relocate?
- Can I visit the school?

You also will need to determine whether you can afford to relocate. A school may be in your state but not in your town. Can you afford moving expenses? Can you afford a place of your own? Does the school have dormitories where you may live at a lower price? (Most small schools don't.) If you want to attend an out-of-state school, you should expect your tuition to double. Before you apply to any school, be sure to visit it to find out if it fits your needs.

- What kind of certification or degree do I want to complete?
- Would I rather train in a hospital, private group practice, or nursing home?
- Where do I want to work?
- What sorts of people do I want to help? (children, adolescents, adults, seniors)
- What salary range do I want?
- What sort of coworkers do I want?

These questions are very important because they will help determine what kind of job you will train for. You should research career options by visiting hospitals, physician practices, and other health organizations in your area to experience the work environment and meet some workers. If you discover you want to train and work in a hospital, you may not be interested in becoming a dental assistant. Also, research the salary range for the job you want at health centers in your area; the salary descriptions in chapter one are not region-specific.

While it's important to set goals for your career, be open to trying or researching work environments that you might not have originally considered. There's also no need to lock yourself into anything permanent after you finish school. You may decide to further your education so you can reach a higher status and salary. Or after becoming, say, a pediatric medical assistant, you may find you don't work well with children and decide you'd rather work with adults.

A registered nurse from Pompton Lakes, New Jersey, says:

> I was lucky I entered healthcare because I'm good at it. When I began as a nursing assistant, though, I didn't know that. I began in orthopedics and then decided pediatrics looked like fun. I tried being in the birthing room and didn't like it; then I tried taking care of the babies and didn't like that either. I had gone back to school and worked part time to become a registered nurse with an associate degree. I had a friend in the surgery recovery room, so I traded a shift with her to try that. I liked surgery, and I've been in here for

fifteen years. Don't assume you will stay with what you have chosen. You may discover open roads once you're working.

Certification is required for many, but not all, health careers, depending on the regulations of the state in which you live and the type of training program you are considering. When you sign up for a particular training program, you will learn the requirements. Usually, after you graduate you will take the state or national certification examinations before going on to employment.

ENTRANCE REQUIREMENTS

Depending on the program and school you attend, you may have to complete an entrance exam such as the Science Placement Test (SPT), the Hobbit Exam, or the College Placement Test (CPT) to determine your placement in courses. These tests evaluate your reading, writing, and math skills. If, for example, you score low in math and high in science, you may be placed in a remedial math course such as Math 099 as review before you take Math 101. Some schools also require Allied Health Entrance Exams such as the Allied Health Aptitude Test (AHAT) for entrance into community college healthcare programs and the Allied Health Profession Aptitude Test (AHPAT) for entrance into four-year colleges. These tests help identify qualified applicants by measuring general academic abilities and scientific knowledge.

Other criteria used in admitting applicants to programs includes the Scholastic Assessment Test (SAT), which you may have taken in high school, the American College Test (ACT), other reading, writing, or science placement tests, grade point average, recommendations and personal statements, and exams specific to certain fields, such as the Nursing School Entrance Exam or the Pharmacy College Admissions Test (PCAT).

Some schools also require a physical and blood work to check for contagious diseases. Students also may have to purchase health insurance if they are not already covered. The school should offer a liability or malpractice insurance policy at a small fee to students and explain the coverage.

TYPES OF TRAINING

Educational requirements for the health occupations discussed in this book generally range from three- to six-month or one-year certificate programs to two years of college. Training for entry-level positions is offered in high schools, vocational-technical centers, community colleges, universities, hospitals, nursing homes, and the Armed Forces, depending on the type of program you are seeking. Most programs provide both classroom and clinical instruction.

High School Programs for Non-Graduated Students

If you haven't graduated from high school or received your GED yet, and you are under 20 years old, your area school district may have a Youth Apprenticeship program designed just for you. It is also for students in grades 10 to 12 who want to pursue healthcare careers. Apprenticeship programs combine with appropriate governmental and social service agencies to help students gain structured school- and work-based learning that leads to a high school diploma, post-secondary credential, or certificate of occupational skills along with social skills and aptitudes needed for success in any job situation. Healthcare programs work with hospitals to open avenues to higher education and certifiable occupations, which will offer students better jobs with higher wages.

School districts offer other programs such as Tech Prep, Cooperative Education, Internships, Explorations in Technology, and Micro Society. These programs may vary from state to state, but they all offer educational skills to apply in real-life healthcare employment situations. Call your local school district for more information.

Certificate Programs

Certificate programs are usually three- to six-month or six-month to one-year programs, and graduates receive a certificate of completion. Entrance requirements include a high school diploma or its equivalent, and entrance exams may be required. Courses combine classroom theory with clinical instruction. Certificate programs differ in that students attend the program straight through, with no breaks except holidays.

Each school has a different set of class names and descriptions, but the basic information you need to learn remains the same. You can find programs at technical schools or community colleges and certificates or degrees for almost every area of healthcare at different levels. A training program is worth considering if it is accredited, if you can commit to the time, and if the subject is one you want to learn. As you can see from the tuition descriptions for each program listed below, being an in-state student is much easier on the wallet; the tuition doubles and sometimes triples for out-of-state students.

Three certificate training programs are described below to give you an idea of what you can expect to find in a training program near you.

Nursing Assistant Sample Courses

Curriculum for certificate programs varies among schools and programs. For example, a one-quarter, three-month certificate course in a nursing assistant program from Big Bend Community College in Moses Lake, Washington, includes:

> **NUR 100 Nursing Assistant**—To prepare nursing assistants for competency as outlined by federal and Washington State curricula. Introduction to healthcare and nursing using classroom, laboratory, self-directed study, and observational experiences.

> **NUR 105 Nursing Trends Laboratory**—Taken concurrently with the nursing assistant core course. The campus laboratory is designed to allow the nursing student to gain proficiency in nursing skills prior to delivering nursing care within a healthcare facility.

As in many other training programs of this kind, the certificate requires only two classes, but the classes take up the whole quarter and are full time. The tuition is $48.60 per quarter hour for in-state students and $190.10 per hour for out-of-state students. The program requires 70 to 80 hours total. Insurance and a work-study program are provided.

At Big Bend Community College, completion of a one-quarter, three-month nursing assistant program entitles you to take the State Certification Examination. Successful completion of the examination is required to become a certified nursing assistant. This program is approved by Aging and Adult Services Administration in Washington State. (Programs and certification vary by state.)

Surgical Technologist Sample Courses

The following course descriptions are from a one-year certificate program in surgical technology at Temple Junior College in Temple, Texas:

> **STTE 1301 Introduction to Surgical Technology**—Includes the history and legal aspects of surgery, psychology of adjustment, environmental control, patient care in pre-operative, intraoperative, and post-operative periods.

All About Training Programs

> **STTE 1202 Surgical Terminology**—Analysis of basic work structure and development of a medical vocabulary related to the body and its systems.
>
> **STTE 1603 Human Structure and Function**—Structure and function of the human body with special emphasis on anatomical structures related to surgical intervention.

Courses will vary by school, semester, and availability for a surgical technology certificate.

Tuition at Temple Community College is $75 per hour for in-state students and $101 per hour for out-of-state students. The program requires 52 hours total. (Program hour length varies by program and school.) Liability insurance is provided by the school. After graduation, students take the National Certified Exam to be certified as surgical technologists. This program is accredited by the Association of Surgical Technologists and the American Medical Association. Some colleges also offer an associate degree for surgical technologists.

Dental Assistant Sample Courses

Here is a partial course description of a twelve-month certificate program in dental assisting from Chemekta Community College in Salem, Oregon:

> **BI060 Basic Science Principles**—Designed for dental assisting and hospitality systems management students. Presents introductory concepts of cell biology, microbiology, chemistry, and physics as applied to specific topics. Includes practical application of problem solving, scientific observation and measurement, use of equipment, and basic laboratory techniques.
>
> **DEN050 Dental Sciences I**—A study of the sciences with the practice of dentistry. Includes oral microbiology, oral pathology, sterilization and disinfection principles, OSHA pathogen, anesthesia, dental office emergencies, and pharmacology.
>
> **DEN051 Introductory Concepts in Dental Assisting**—Designed to introduce the student to basic general and oral anatomy. Particular attention directed toward physiological processes of the body, the oral cavity and its associated structures, and anatomical terminology.

Courses will vary by school and availability for the dental assisting program.

Tuition at Chemeketa Community College is $35 per hour for in-state students and $121 per hour for out-of-state students; however, after 90 days the tuition rate for out-of-state students drops to the same as for in-state students. The program requires 52 hours total. Liability insurance is provided by the school, and work-study is available. Program graduates take the Dental Assisting National Board Examinations to be certified as dental assistants. This course is accredited by the American Dental Association Commission. An associate degree in dental assisting is also available at many schools.

Associate Degree Programs

An associate degree program requires two academic or two calendar years. Entrance requirements include a high school diploma or a GED, and some programs require college prep courses. Most associate degree programs require entrance and placement exams. In an associate degree program, half the required courses are in liberal arts and half are in the major. Courses in the major combine classroom theory with clinical practice in extended care facilities, hospitals, and community agencies.

The benefit of receiving a two-year associate degree is the combination of liberal arts classes with medical classes, as well as the opportunity for a better job and higher pay. Also, colleges have clubs and organizations that offer students valuable life experience. While attending a college, participate in as many campus activities as you can; don't restrict yourself to activities related to your major. One nursing student from Orlando, Florida, shares some advice:

> The best thing I ever did was take an acting class. I know that acting doesn't have anything to do with being a nursing assistant, but it gave me an outlet so I didn't feel confined to biology and labs. I didn't want my whole school career to be nursing, but I knew I wouldn't become a famous actress either. I met some interesting people, and the class was a lot of fun. The acting class gave me a break from the daily routine of health and also helped me as I trained to work with people.

Radiologic Technologist Sample Courses

A radiologic technology associate degree from Athens Technical Institute in Athens, Georgia, requires the following types of courses:

All About Training Programs

General Education

ENG 191 Composition and Rhetoric—Expository themes in both general and medical topics developed by basic rhetorical methods. Effective writing techniques.

MAT 191 College Algebra—A study of algebra, including absolute values and inequalities, complex numbers, functions including polynomial, rational, exponential and logarithmic functions, systems of equations, and the binomial theorem.

Radiologic Technology Major

RAD 101 Introduction to Radiography—Provides an overview of radiography, patient care, and the profession as a whole with emphasis on patient care with consideration of both physical and psychological conditions. Topics include ethics, medical and legal consideration, professionalism, basic principles of radiation protection, basic principles of exposure, equipment, hospital and departmental organizations, body mechanics, vital signs, medical emergencies, contrast agents, CPR, and death and dying.

RAD 107 Principles of Radiographic Exposure I—Introduces factors that govern and influence the production of the radiographic image on radiographic film. Lab demonstrations. Topics include radiographic density, contrast, recorded detail, distortion, exposure latitude, film holders, processing, handling and storage, and state and federal regulations.

Courses will vary by school, semester, and availability for an associate degree in radiologic technology.

At Athens Technical Institute, full-time students pay $283 in fees each quarter. Part-time students pay $21 per credit hour. The radiologic technologist associate degree requires 139 hours total. Insurance is provided by the school, and graduates are eligible to sit for the National Certification Examination. The program is accredited by the Commission on Accreditation for Allied Health Education Programs.

Medical Assistant Sample Courses

Here is an example of the course curriculum for an associate degree in medical assisting from Pitt Community College in Greenville, North Carolina:

General Education

CAS 100 Introduction to Microcomputer Applications—General introduction to the microcomputer, DOS, and various software application packages, including word processing, spreadsheets, and database management.

OSC 110 Word Processing—Software program developed for use on the MS-DOS microcomputer. Designed to give the student a basic understanding of the WP software and the operation and application of the microcomputer through classroom instruction and hands-on experience.

Medical Assisting Major

BIO 101 Basic Anatomy and Physiology—Foundation of facts and principles in the normal structure and related functioning of the following body systems: skeletal, muscular, digestive, circulatory, respiratory, urinary, reproductive, endocrine, integumentary, nervous, and special sense organs. Presents principles and concepts of physiology and immunology.

BIO 101A Basic Anatomy and Physiology Laboratory—Laboratory setting presents the student with a foundation of facts and principles in the normal structure and related functioning of the human body.

Courses will vary by school, semester, and availability.

Tuition at Pitt Community College is $20 per hour for in-state students and $163 per hour for out-of-state students. The program requires 109 hours total. Malpractice insurance is available from the school, and work-study is available. After graduation, students are required to complete an application to the American Association of Medical Assistants to take the Medical Assisting Certification Examination. A certificate course is also available at some schools for the medical assistant program.

Physical Therapist Assistant Sample Courses

Here is a sampling of the course curriculum of the physical therapist assistant program at Volunteer State Community College in Gallatin, Tennessee:

General Education

ENG101 Composition and Rhetoric—Emphasizes the development and improvement of written and oral communication abilities.

MAT131 College Algebra—Emphasizes problem-solving techniques. Topics include fundamental algebra concepts and operations, linear and quadratic equations and functions, simultaneous equations, inequalities, exponents and powers, graphing techniques, and word problems.

Physical Therapist Assistant Major

BIO231 Human Anatomy and Physiology I—Introduces the structure and function of the body as a whole and studies of the integumentary (skin), skeletal, muscular, nervous, sensory, and endocrine systems.

BIO232 Human Anatomy and Physiology II—Studies the structure and function of the following body systems: blood, lymphatic, cardiovascular, respiratory, digestive, urinary, and reproductive.

PTA110 Physical Science for the Physical Therapist Assistant—Focuses on basic, normal structure and function of the human body. Topics include an overview of each body system and how systems coordinate activities to maintain a balanced state, recognizing deviations from the normal.

Courses will vary by school, semester, and availability.

Tuition at Volunteer State Community College is $48 per hour for in-state students and $190 per hour for out-of-state students. The program requires 109 hours total. Malpractice insurance is available through the school. Graduates are required to pass the appropriate state examinations for a physical therapist assistant license. This course is accredited by the Committee on Accreditation for Physical Therapist Assistants.

Baccalaureate Programs

The bachelor degree program combines major courses with general education in a four-year curriculum in a college or university. You may be admitted to your major program as a freshman or after one or two years of general education or liberal arts courses at another institution. If you go to a small college or technical school to become a surgical technician with an associate degree, and then decide after about a year that you want to move on to a higher degree and level of salary, you can always go back to school to obtain a bachelor's degree.

A high school diploma or its equivalent (GED) is required for admission, and placement exams, SAT scores, ACT scores, and an acceptable high school

GPA may be required. Entrance requirements may be more competitive than for shorter training programs. You may have to take a higher level of tests to enter the specific major area, such as the Allied Health Aptitude Test or the Dental Admissions Test. Because a bachelor's degree requires at least four years of school if you don't already have some schooling, you may, like most students, require some financial aid.

Attending college for several years is not for everyone, so be sure that the health occupation you choose doesn't require more training than you are willing to commit yourself to. On the other hand, don't write a college education off for financial reasons. Remember, there are scholarships and loans, plus a number of other ways to help pay for college. (See chapter four for details about financial aid.)

Work-Study Programs

Regardless of which training program you select, you should consult your career counselor or advisor to see if your school has a work-study program. Work-study programs provide assistance for full-time students who need additional financial aid, though you may earn only minimum wage. Work hours—no more than 20 hours per week—do not compete with class hours, and students gain extra work experience in the process. Work-study programs are provided on a need-based basis. This is a good way to experience a professional work environment and the associated responsibilities.

Internships

One of the best ways to gain practical job skills is through an internship in which you can experience a professional work environment in your chosen field. To begin your search for an internship, consult your school's career development, counseling, or internship offices. Let your counselor know what you're looking for. If you are looking for a paid internship, your choices will be significantly fewer; most internships are unpaid. Remember that the experience you gain could lead to a full-time position.

Companies across the nation provide internships for prospective healthcare students. For example, the American Heart Association offers 250 to 300 internships a year for summer programs, as well as one-semester and one-year terms. The internships are offered nationwide, and grants are available as well. The March of Dimes offers a flexible number of part-time and year-round internships. Many other organizations offer internships, including the

All About Training Programs

Leukemia Society of America, the American Cancer Society, the American Red Cross, and other smaller companies like Action AIDS. For more information on these associations, see your counselor and Appendix A under *Internships*.

CHOOSING THE RIGHT TRAINING PROGRAM

You should find out all you can about the school(s) you want to attend. Finding out the details will save time, money, and energy in the long run. Here are some tough questions to ask about each training program:

- What requirements must I meet?

You may be required to take English, math, or science placement tests to be considered for your training program. You may also need to take the SAT or ACT if you have not already taken one of these in high school.

- Is the program I chose accredited? By whom?

Accreditation is very important; it tells you the school offers high-quality education. Many agencies accredit programs in every field of the healthcare industry. Don't be overwhelmed by the number of accrediting associations. Just be sure your targeted school lists one or more of them as its accrediting agency.

Tips on Applying to Programs

- Apply as early as you can. You'll need to fill out an application, submit official high school or GED transcripts, and any copies of SAT, ACT, or other test scores used for admission. If you haven't taken these, you may have to before you can be admitted. Call the school and find out when the next program starts, then apply at least a month or two prior to make sure you can complete requirements before the program starts.
- You will receive a prewritten request for transcripts from the admissions office when you get your application. Make sure you send those requests as soon as possible, so the admissions process is not held up in any way.
- Make the earliest possible appointment to take any placement tests that may be required, so they do not hold up admissions.
- Pay your fees before the deadline. Enrollment is not complete each quarter or semester until the student has paid all fees by the date specified on the registration form. If fees are not paid by the deadline, the classes will be canceled. If you are going to receive financial aid, apply as early as you can to prevent fee default.
- Find out if you must pass a physical or have any other medical history forms on file for the school you choose, so this does not hold up admissions.

For example, the American Association of Medical Assistants (AAMA) Curriculum Review Board (CRB) assesses the quality of programs seeking accreditation for medical assistant technology. It then advises the Council on Accreditation and Unit Recognition (CAUR) of the Commission on Accreditation for Allied Health Education Programs (CAAHEP) as to whether the program should be accredited.

The Commission on Accreditation of Allied Health Education Programs (CAAHEP) and the Accrediting Bureau of Health Education Schools (ABHES) are both recognized by the U.S. Department of Education for accrediting such programs. For a list of associations that maintain lists or directories on accredited programs, see Appendix A under *Accrediting Organizations.*

- What are the faculty members' qualifications? How experienced are they?

The program should include some faculty members with advanced degrees (M.S., M.D., M.B.A., D.D.S., D.O., and so on) and some with significant experience in the working world (at least five to seven years). The faculty should be accessible for student conferences.

- What percentage of graduates were placed in jobs upon graduation? Is there a career placement office or a counselor/advisor on campus?

The placement rate for graduates is extremely important, and when considering a school, whether small or large, you should ask about it. Many schools offer free placement services for the working lifetime of their graduates.

- Is the school equipped with the latest technology?

Again, always visit the school you plan to attend, and ask to see the laboratory facilities and equipment. The most recent and advanced computer technology and training equipment should be available to students.

MAKING THE MOST OF A TRAINING PROGRAM

After you enter a training program to receive a certificate or degree, you want to make the most of your training experience, right? The rest of this chapter shows you how to maximize the learning process. Apply the tips listed below to get the most out of your training program.

All About Training Programs

How to Study for Exams

Remember studying for exams in high school? No matter what your IQ, studying is crucial to success in a career training program, where the work is much tougher than in high school. However, don't let the word *exam* make you nervous. Exams are the instructor's way of finding out what you learned and what you may need to review before going any further with assignments. You must remember every technique you learn and be able to apply the experience to real life. That means studying is extremely important. A radiology instructor from Athens Technical Institute in Athens, Georgia, says:

> Some of the rad tech program involves reviewing the anatomy you have to demonstrate on radiograms. Some is positioning. Some studying is strictly academic, such as going over your notes from class, reading the chapter, and writing down key points. Studying depends mostly on the type of course you have. We have labs that review much of the information learned in class. However, learning anatomy requires memorization, and if you're not good at memorization, you may have to study more than others do.

Some instructors will tell you to study at least two hours for each hour of class. This may seem difficult and time-consuming, but there are ways to make it easier, including reviewing your notes, reading appropriate textbook chapters, studying with others, and studying between classes.

If you remain on task in classes and labs and review steadily, you should have no problem with exams. Many exams are multiple choice, and the wrong answers may point you to the correct answer. Essay exams require you to write more information than a regular multiple choice test can ask for. Your instructor may clue you in to what format he or she will use, so you can study accordingly. During the test, remember to read the instructions carefully and listen to your instructor's directions.

How to Take Notes in Class

Taking good notes in class will help you to study after class. Listen attentively and try to write down the most important information. Many instructors indicate what you should write down and what is already in the book you will be studying. If an instructor writes anything on the board or on an overhead, you should write it too. Writing down too much information is better than writing too little, but be sure you are listening to the instructor as well as taking notes. A medical assistant instructor from Santa Barbara Business School, California, says:

> The problem most students have is they try to write down everything that's said, a laundry list of things. What they need to do is listen for key points and concepts, and the textbook will have all the little details that they can go back and read. It's a good idea to read the chapter before you come to class, so you know what's in there and have questions ready for the instructor. And supplement your note-taking. Make a note about something you didn't understand well when you read it or be prepared to ask questions that could set the tone for the lecture.

Rewriting your notes from each class helps you sort out the needed information and helps reinforce the information discussed in class.

Studying With Other Students

Studying with other students is one of the best ways to learn. Teaching another person can help you to learn and remember the material. Also, having someone quiz you or explain something that you don't understand makes the information more real and less boring. Create a study group or join one, and together with classmates massage your knowledge of your particular program. An Athens, Georgia resident radiology instructor says:

> We have small, limited classes, so we try to pick people we feel will best succeed. They shouldn't be competitive but should be supportive of each other. Small study groups really help reinforce things. Another thing we do is labs, where students position each other like patients in the hospital. Basically, they have to work together, interacting in the clinic and labs, so they get to know each other and have their own war stories to tell each other. Study groups are really a good idea.

Also, in case you didn't take very good notes or missed a day of class, your fellow students can come to your rescue. Of course, you shouldn't miss any classes if you can help it.

Getting to Know Your Instructor

The first thing you should do after entering a class is make an appointment to meet with the instructor so you can ask questions, get to know him or her, and find out what's expected of you. Each instructor is different and has different expectations. Also, if you have a child at home or some problem that might take time away from the class, you can inform the instructor ahead of time.

In the clinical classes, you may have the opportunity to get to know instructors personally while working directly with them. Many instructors work one-on-one with students in the most difficult part of the program to make sure they understand the procedures and instructions, become oriented, and really learn that procedure. Instructors may go with you to the hospital or clinic where you will receive additional clinical education.

Using the Career Planning and Placement Office

Most schools have a career planning and placement office. Make an appointment right away to meet with a counselor in your field so you can begin working on a plan for job hunting before your graduation or certificate release. Your counselor will help you build your resume, tell you about job prospects in your area of specialization, and perhaps set up a placement file that allows you to send resume information directly from the school.

Career centers offer a variety of career-advising activities, such as one-on-one sessions in which students and advisors discuss effective career decision-making preferences, interests, values, and other concerns. Establishing goals is an important part of these sessions. You can make an appointment at any time throughout your training program if you have questions about your future career. Other services offered may include a career services library, a videotape library, a Career and Life Development workshop, an information line/job vacancy hotline, internship programs, student employment services, career days, workshops, and mock and on-campus interviews. Each school is different, so career placement programs and services will vary. A career planning and placement counselor in New Orleans, Louisiana, has this advice:

> The Career Planning and Placement Center is our way of reaching out to assist you in your search for suitable employment. How much you benefit from our services is up to you and your desire to find a career that fits your personality, abilities, and skills. Many people get stuck in

a job they don't like because they didn't take the time to research the job. Make the career center at your school of choice one of your primary resources as you move toward your career goals.

If you don't take advantage of your school's career placement service, you may wind up paying large fees to a private employment agency after you graduate.

THE INSIDE TRACK

Who:	Lisa Williams
What:	Medical technologist
Where:	Summit Medical Center, Frisco, Colorado
How long:	Two years
How much:	$30,000 annual salary
Degree:	Bachelor's degree in medical technology
School:	Medical College of Georgia, Augusta, Georgia

Insider's Advice

I knew I wanted to do something in the medical field, and I knew nursing was not really up my alley. I called and requested information from medical schools around Georgia and read about the programs they offered. When I read about the medical technologist degree, I knew that was what I wanted to do. I could learn about five different lab areas without having to specialize in only one of them. The areas I work in are hematology, chemistry, microbiology, immunology, and blood bank.

Because I wasn't sure what I wanted to do, I researched my options. I found an accredited program and pursued my future career. Deciding on a career is not easy, but once you find something you like, stick with it and work hard. I decided to get my bachelor's degree because I had the time, and I received financial aid grants and loans to help with expenses. I am currently finishing paying off my student loans, and I am happy about the way I made my career decision.

Insider's Take on the Future

I plan to go back to school soon. I would like to one day receive my Ph.D., but I haven't decided in which field. It will either be immunology or pathology. I'm looking at another four to six years of school. I'm not sure where I will attend school because I would still like to move back to Georgia, where my family lives; I will have to research more schools. My ideal future job would be working as a doctor for the Center for Disease Control in Atlanta, helping to discover cures.

CHAPTER 3

DIRECTORY OF HEALTHCARE TRAINING PROGRAMS

This chapter contains a directory of technical and career schools, proprietary and vocational schools, independent colleges, and other schools that offer training programs for the healthcare jobs discussed in this book. All programs provide school name, address, and phone number, so you can contact each school directly to get more information and application forms for the programs that interest you.

Now that you've decided to get into a training program, you need to find one at a school near you. First locate the job title you want, and then look under the state to find the schools in that area. The schools are listed in alphabetical order by city within each state, so you can quickly locate schools in nearby cities. Although the schools included in this chapter are not endorsed or recommended by LearningExpress, this list is intended to help you begin your search for an appropriate school by offering a representative listing of accredited schools in each state. Since so many schools offer healthcare programs, not all could be listed here due to space limitations. However, this representative listing should get you started. Appendix A includes names of professional associations you can write to for additional lists of accredited training programs in your area.

DENTAL ASSISTANT TECHNOLOGY

ALABAMA
Community College of the Air Force
Maxwell Air Force Base
Montgomery 36112
334-953-6436

ARIZONA
Apollo College-Tri City, Inc.
630 West Southern Ave.
Mesa 85210
602-831-6585

Institute of Medical and Dental Technology
20 East Main St.
Mesa 85201
602-969-5505

The Bryman School
4343 North 16th St.
Phoenix 85016
602-274-4300

Apollo College-Phoenix, Inc.
8503 North 27th Ave.
Phoenix 85015
602-864-1571

The Laural School
2538 North Eighth St.
Phoenix 85006
602-947-6565

Apollo College
3870 North Oracle Rd.
Tucson 85705
520-888-5885

CALIFORNIA
Southern California College of Medical-Dental Care
1717 South Brookhurst St.
Anaheim 92804
714-635-3450

San Joaquin Valley College
201 New Stine Rd.
Bakersfield 93309
805-834-0126

Orange Coast College
2701 Fairview Rd.
Costa Mesa 92626
714-432-0202

Galen College of Medical and Dental Assistants
1325 North Wishon Ave.
Fresno 93728
209-264-9726

San Joaquin Valley College
3333 North Bond
Fresno 93726
209-229-7800

Citrus College
1000 West Foothill Blvd.
Glendora 91741-1899
818-914-8516

Huntington College of Dental Technology
7466 Edinger Ave.
Huntington Beach 92647
714-841-9500

Bryman College
5350 Atlantic Ave.
Long Beach 90805
310-422-6007

Donald Vocational School
1833 West Eighth St.
Los Angeles 90057
310-483-2080

Nova Institute of Health Technology
2400 South Western Ave.
Los Angeles 90018
213-735-2222

Directory of Healthcare Programs

Galen College of Medical and Dental Assistants
1604 Ford Ave.
Modesto 95350
209-527-5084

Concorde Career Institute
4150 Lankershim Blvd.
North Hollywood 91602
818-766-8151

Nova Institute of Health Technology
520 North Euclid Ave.
Ontario 91762
909-984-5027

Institute of Business and Medical Technology
75-110 Saint Charles Place
Palm Desert 92260
619-776-5873

Diablo Valley College
321 Golf Club Rd.
Pleasant Hill 94523
510-685-1230

Bryman College
3505 North Hart Ave.
Rosemead 91770
818-573-5470

Concorde Career Institute
570 West 4th St.
San Bernardino 92401
909-884-8891

Concorde Career Institute
123 Camino De La Reina
San Diego 92108
619-688-0800

Bryman College
731 Markey St.
San Francisco 94103
415-777-2500

Concorde Career Institute
1290 North First St.
San Jose 92108
408-441-6411

Western Career College
170 Bay Fair Mall
San Leandro 94578
510-278-3888

Allan Hancock College
800 South College Dr.
Santa Maria 93454
805-922-6966

Santa Rosa Junior College
1501 Mendocino Ave.
Santa Rosa 95401-4395
707-527-4100

Concorde Career Institute
6850 Van Nuys Blvd.
Van Nuys 91405
818-780-5252

Galen College of Medical and Dental Assistants
3746 West Mineral King
Visalia 93277
209-732-2217

San Joaquin Valley College
8400 West Mineral King Ave.
Visalia 93291
209-651-2500

Nova Institute of Health Technology
11416 Whittier Rd.
Whittier 90601
213-695-0771

Bryman College
20835 Sherman Way
Winnetka 91306
818-887-7911

COLORADO

Concorde Career Institute
770 Grant St.
Denver 80203
303-861-1151

Heritage College of Health Careers
12 Lakeside Ln.
Denver 80212
303-477-7240

Front Range Community College
3645 West 112th Ave.
Westminster 80030
303-466-8811

CONNECTICUT

Huntington Institute, Inc.
193 Broadway
Norwich 06360
203-886-0507

FLORIDA

Concorde Career Institute
7960 Arlington Expwy.
Jacksonville 32211
904-725-0525

Florida Community College at Jacksonville
501 West State St.
Jacksonville 32202
904-632-3000

Palm Beach Community College
4200 Congress Ave.
Lake Worth 33461
407-967-7222

Southern College
5600 Lake Underhill Rd.
Orlando 32807
407-273-1000

Concorde Career Institute
4202 West Spruce St.
Tampa 33607
813-874-0094

GEORGIA

Albany Technical Institute
1021 Lowe Rd.
Albany 31708
912-430-3520

Atlanta College of Medical Dental Careers
1240 West Peachtree St. NE
Atlanta 30309-2906
404-249-8200

Medix Schools
2480 Windy Hill Rd.
Marietta 30067
770-980-0002

IDAHO

American Institute of Health Technology, Inc.
6600 Emerald
Boise 83704
208-377-8080

ILLINOIS

Kaskaskia College
27210 College Rd.
Centralia 62801
618-532-1981

Parkland College
2400 West Bradley Ave.
Champaign 61821
217-351-2200

VIP Schools, Inc.
600 N. McClurg Court
Chicago 60611-3044
312-266-1484

Directory of Healthcare Programs

INDIANA
Indiana University–Purdue University at Indianapolis
355 North Lansing
Indianapolis 46202
317-274-5555

Professional Career Institute
2611 Waterfront Pkwy., East Dr.
Indianapolis 46214-2028
317-299-6001

KANSAS
Bryan Institute
1004 South Oliver
Wichita 67218
316-685-2284

LOUISIANA
Domestic Health Care Institute
4826 Jamestown Ave.
Baton Rouge 70808
504-925-5312

Delta Schools, Inc.
4549 Johnston Dr.
Lafayette 70503
318-988-2211

Eastern College of Health Vocation
3540 I-10 Service Rd. S.
Metairie 70001
504-834-8644

Delta Schools, Inc.
413 West Admiral Doyle
New Iberia 70560
318-365-7348

MARYLAND
Medix Schools
1017 York Rd.
Towson 21204-9840
410-337-5155

MASSACHUSETTS
Bryman College
323 Boylston St.
Brookline 02146
617-232-6035

MICHIGAN
Ferris State University
901 South State St.
Big Rapids 49307
616-592-2100

Ross Medical Education Center
1036 Gilbert St.
Flint 48504-5258
810-230-1100

Grand Rapids Community College
143 Bostwick Ave. NE
Grand Rapids 49505
616-771-4000

Grand Rapids Educational Center
1750 Woodworth NE
Grand Rapids 49505
616-364-8464

Ross Medical Education Center
1188 North West Ave.
Jackson 49202
517-782-7677

Grand Rapids Educational Center
5349 West Main
Kalamazoo 49009
616-381-9616

Ross Medical Education Center
913 West Holmes
Lansing 48910
517-887-0180

Ross Medical Education Center
4054 Bay Rd.
Saginaw 48603
517-793-9800

51

Delta College
University Center 48710
517-686-9000

Ross Medical Education Center
26417 Hoover Rd.
Warren 48089
810-758-7200

MINNESOTA
Range Technical College-Hibbing Campus
2900 East Beltline
Hibbing 55746
218-262-6185

Concorde Career Institute, Inc.
12 North 12th St.
Minneapolis 55403
612-341-3850

Lakeland Medical and Dental Academy
1402 West Lake St.
Minneapolis 55408
612-827-5656

Northeast Metro Technical College
3300 Century Ave. N
White Bear Lake 55110
612-779-5827

MISSISSIPPI
Hinds Community College–Raymond Campus
Raymond 39154-9799
601-857-3212

MISSOURI
Concorde Career Institute
3239 Broadway
Kansas City 64111
816-531-5223

Al-Med Academy
10963 Saint Charles Rock Rd.
Saint Louis 63074
314-739-4450

Missouri School for Doctors' Assistants
10121 Manchester Rd.
Saint Louis 63122
314-821-7700

Saint Louis Community College–Forest Park
5600 Oakland Ave.
Saint Louis 63110
314-644-9280

NEVADA
American Academy for Career Education
3120 East Desert Inn Rd.
Las Vegas 89121
702-732-7748

Professional Careers
3305 Spring Mountain Rd.
Las Vegas 89120
702-368-2338

NEW HAMPSHIRE
New Hampshire Technical Institute
11 Institute Dr.
Concord 03301
603-225-1865

NEW JERSEY
Camden County College
P.O. Box 200
Blackwood 08012
609-228-7200

Empire Technical School of New Jersey
576 Central Ave.
East Orange 07018
201-675-0565

Berdan Institute
265 Rte. 46 W.
Totowa 07512
201-256-3444

Directory of Healthcare Programs

NEW YORK
New York School for Medical and Dental Assistants
116-16 Queens Blvd.
Forest Hills 11375
718-793-2330

Mandl School
254 West 54th St.
New York 10019
212-247-3434

Techno-Dent Training Center
101 West 31st St.
New York 10001
212-695-1818

Continental Dental Assistant School
633 Jefferson Rd.
Rochester 14623
716-272-8060

NORTH CAROLINA
Alamance Community College
P.O. Box 8000
Graham 27253
919-578-2002

Guilford Technical Community College
P.O. Box 309
Jamestown 27282
919-334-4822

OHIO
Akron Medical-Dental Institute
733 West Market St.
Akron 44303
216-762-9788

Institute of Medical-Dental Technology
375 Glensprings Dr.
Cincinnati 45246
513-851-8500

Cleveland Institute of Dental-Medical Assistants
1836 Euclid Ave.
Cleveland 44115
216-241-2930

Eastland Career Center
4465 South Hamilton Rd.
Groveport 43125
614-836-3903

Cleveland Institute of Dental-Medical Assistants
5564 Mayfield Rd.
Lyndhurst 44124
216-473-6273

Cleveland Institute of Dental-Medical Assistants
5733 Hopkins Rd.
Mentor 44060
216-946-9530

OKLAHOMA
Metro Tech Vocational Technical Center
1900 Springlake Dr.
Oklahoma City 73111
405-424-8324

Kiamichi AVTS SD #7–Talihina Campus
Rte. 2 & Hwy. 63A, P.O. Box 1800
Talihina 74571
918-567-2264

Bryan Institute
2843 East 51st St.
Tulsa 74105-1709
918-749-6891

OREGON
Lane Community College
4000 East 30th Ave.
Eugene 97405
503-747-4501

Apollo College–Portland, Inc.
2600 Southeast 98th Ave.
Portland 97266
503-761-6100

College of America
921 Southwest Washington
Portland 97205
503-242-9000

Portland Community College
P.O. Box 19000
Portland 97280-0990
503-244-6111

PENNSYLVANIA
Academy of Medical Arts and Business
279 Boas St.
Harrisburg 17102
717-233-2172

Career Training Academy
703 Fifth Ave.
New Kensington 15068
412-337-1000

Community College of Philadelphia
1700 Spring Garden St.
Philadelphia 19130
215-715-8000

Delaware Valley Academy of Medical and Dental Assistants
3330 Grant Ave.
Philadelphia 19149
215-676-1200

Median School of Allied Health Careers
125 Seventh St.
Pittsburgh 15222-3400
800-570-0693

RHODE ISLAND
Community College of Rhode Island
400 East Ave.
Warwick 02886-1805
401-825-1000

TENNESSEE
Chattanooga State Technical Community College
4501 Amnicola Hwy.
Chattanooga 37406
615-697-4401

Memphis Area Vocational-Technical School
550 Alabama Ave.
Memphis 38105-3799
901-543-6100

Shelbyville State Area Vocational Technical School
1405 Madison St.
Shelbyville 37160
615-685-5013

TEXAS
Bryan Institute
1719 Pioneer Pkwy. W
Arlington 76013
817-265-5588

Allied Health Careers
5424 Hwy. 290 W
Austin 78735
512-892-5210

ATI Health Education Center
8150 Brookriver Dr.
Dallas 75247
214-637-0980

Career Centers of Texas El Paso, Inc.
8375 Burnham Dr.
El Paso 79907
915-595-1935

ATI Health Education Center
1200 Summit Ave.
Fort Worth 76102
817-429-1045

Directory of Healthcare Programs

San Antonio College of Medical and
Dental Assistants–South
3900 North 23rd
McAllen 78501
210-630-1499

San Antonio College of Medical and
Dental Assistants–Central
4205 San Pedro Ave.
San Antonio 76212
210-733-0777

Texas State Technical College–Waco
Campus
3801 Campus Dr.
Waco 76705
817-867-3371

UTAH
American Institute of Medical-Dental
Technology
1675 North 200 West
Provo 84604
801-377-2900

Provo College
1450 West 820 North
Provo 84601
801-375-1861

Bryman School
1144 West 3300 South
Salt Lake City 84119-3330
801-975-7000

VIRGINIA
Career Development Center
605 Thimble Shoals
Newport News 23606
804-599-4088

Riverside Regional Medical Center–
School of Professional Nursing
500 J. Clyde Morris Blvd.
Newport News 23601
804-594-2700

National Business College
1813 East Main St.
Salem 24153
540-986-1800

WASHINGTON
Bellingham Technical College
3028 Lindbergh Ave.
Bellingham 98225
360-738-0221

Eton Technical Institute
31919 Sixth Ave. S
Federal Way 98063
206-941-5800

Lake Washington Technical College
11605 132nd Ave. NE
Kirkland 98034
206-828-5600

Eton Technical Institute
3659 Frontage Rd.
Port Orchard 98366
206-479-3866

Seattle Vocational Institute
315 22nd Ave. S
Seattle 98144
206-587-4950

Spokane Community College
North 1810 Greene Ave.
Spokane 99207
509-533-7000

Trend College
North 214 Wall St.
Spokane 99201
509-838-3521

Bates Technical College
1101 South Yakima Ave.
Tacoma 98405
206-596-1500

WISCONSIN

Fox Valley Technical College
1825 North Bluemound Dr.
Appleton 54913-2277
414-735-5600

Western Wisconsin Technical College
304 North Sixth St., P.O. Box 908
La Crosse 54602-0908
608-785-9200

MEDICAL ASSISTANT TECHNOLOGY

ALABAMA

Gadsden Business College
P.O. Box 1575
Anniston 36202-1575
205-237-7517

New World College of Business
P.O. Box 2287
Anniston 36201
205-236-7578

George C. Wallace State
College–Dotham
Rte. 6, P.O. Box 62
Dotham 36303-9234
334-983-3521

Gadsden Business College
750 Forest Ave.
Gadsden 35901
205-546-2863

Capps College
3100 Cottage Hill Rd.
Montgomery 36606
205-473-1393

Coastal Training Institute
5950 Monticello Dr.
Montgomery 36112
205-279-6241

Community College of the Air Force
Maxwell Air Force Base
Montgomery 36112
334-953-6436

ARIZONA

Apollo College–Tri City, Inc.
630 West Southern Ave.
Mesa 85210
602-831-6585

Institute of Medical and Dental
Technology
20 East Main St.
Mesa 85201
602-969-5505

Apollo College–Phoenix, Inc.
8503 North 27th Ave.
Phoenix 85051
602-864-1571

Apollo College–Westridge, Inc.
7502 West Thomas Rd.
Phoenix 85033
602-849-9000

The Bryman School
4343 North 16th St.
Phoenix 85016
602-274-4300

Gateway Community College
108 North 40th St.
Phoenix 85034
602-392-5189

The Laural School
2538 North 8th St.
Phoenix 85006
602-947-6565

Occupational Training Center
4136 North 75th Ave.
Phoenix 85033
602-849-0308

Directory of Healthcare Programs

Apollo College
3870 North Oracle Rd.
Tucson 85705
520-888-5885

Pima Medical Institute
3350 East Grant Rd.
Tucson 85710
520-326-1600

ARKANSAS
Eastern College of Health Vocation
6423 Forbing Rd.
Little Rock 72209
501-568-0211

CALIFORNIA
Advanced Computer Training
3467 W. Shaw
Fresno 93703
209-277-1900

American College of Optechs
4021 Rosewood Ave.
Los Angeles 90004
310-383-2862

DISTRICT OF COLUMBIA
Harrison Center for Career Education
624 Ninth St. NW
Washington 20001
202-628-5672

FLORIDA
William T. McFatter Vocational Technical Center
6500 Nova Dr.
Davie 33317
954-370-8324

Keiser College of Technology
1500 Northwest 49th St.
Fort Lauderdale 33309
305-776-4456

Santa Fe Community College
3000 Northwest 83rd St.
Gainesville 32601
904-395-5000

Concorde Career Institute
7960 Arlington Expwy.
Jacksonville 32211
904-725-0525

Concorde Career Institute
4000 North State Rd.
Lauderdale Lake 33319
954-731-8880

Career Training Institute
101 West Main St.
Leesburg 34748
904-326-5134

Phillips Junior College
2401 North Harbor City Blvd.
Melbourne 32935
407-254-6459

Martin Technical College
1901 Northwest Seventh St.
Miami 33125
305-541-8140

Miriam Vocational School, Inc.
7311 West Flagler St.
Miami 33144
305-264-1402

National Education Center–Bauder College Campus
7955 Northwest 12th St.
Miami 33126-1823
305-477-0251

Polytechnical Institute of Florida
1405 Southwest 107th Ave.
Miami 33174
305-226-8099

Miami Lakes Technical Education Center
5780 Northwest 158th St.
Miami Lakes 33169
305-557-1100

Webster College, Inc.
5623 U.S. Hwy. 19 S
New Port Richey 34652
813-849-4993

Miami Technical College
14701 Northwest Seventh Ave.
North Miami 33168
305-688-8811

National School of Technology, Inc.
16150 Northeast 17th Ave.
North Miami Beach 33162
305-949-9500

Career Training Institute
2120 West Colonial
Orlando 32804
407-843-3984

Orlando College
5500-5800 Diplomat Circle
Orlando 32810
407-628-5870

Concorde Career Institute
4202 West Spruce St.
Tampa 33602
813-874-0094

Florida School of Business
4817 Florida Ave. N
Tampa 33603
813-239-3334

Ross Technical Institute
1490 South Military Trail
West Palm Beach 33415
407-433-1288

Tampa College
3319 West Hillsborough Ave.
Tampa 33614
813-879-6000

GEORGIA
Meadows College of Business
832 Slappey Blvd.
Albany 31701
912-883-1736

Athens Area Technical Institute
800 Hwy. 29 N
Athens 30601
706-355-5000

Atlanta Area Technical School
1560 Stewart Ave. SW
Atlanta 30310
404-756-3779

Atlanta College of Medical Dental Careers
1240 West Peachtree St. NE
Atlanta 30309-2906
404-880-8500

Draughons College–Atlanta
1430 Peachtree St.
Atlanta 30309
404-892-0814

Bryman College
40 Marietta St. NW
Atlanta 30303
404-524-8800

Augusta Technical Institute
3116 Deans Bridge Rd.
Augusta 30906
706-771-4000

Gwinnett Technical Institute
1250 Atkinson Rd., P.O. Box 1505
Lawrenceville 30246-1505
404-962-7580

LearningExpress

20 Academy Street, P.O. Box 7100, Norwalk, CT 06852-9879

★FREE!★ TEN TIPS TO PASSING ANY TEST

To provide you with the test prep and career information you need, we would appreciate your help. Please answer the following questions and return this postage paid survey. As our Thank You, we will send you our "Ten Tips To Passing Any Test" – surefire ways to score your best on classroom and/or job-related exams.

Name : _____

Address : _____

_____

Age : _____   Sex : ☐ Male   ☐ Female

Highest Level of School Completed : ☐ High School   ☐ College

1) I am currently :

    A student — Year/level: _____

    Employed — Job title: _____

    Other — Please explain: _____

2) Jobs/careers of interest to me are :

    1. _____

    2. _____

    3. _____

3) If you are a student, did your guidance/career counselor provide you with job information/materials? _____

Name & Location of School: _____

_____

_____

_____

4) What newspapers and/or magazines do you subscribe to or read regularly? _____

_____

5) Do you own a computer? _____

   Do you have Internet access? _____

   How often do you go on-line? _____

6) Have you purchased career-related materials from bookstores? _____

If yes, list recent examples: _____

_____

7) Which radio stations do you listen to regularly (please give call letters and city name)?

_____

_____

8) How did you hear about this LearningExpress book?

   An ad? _____

   If so, where? _____

   An order form in the back of another book? _____

   A recommendation? _____

   A bookstore? _____

   Other? _____

9) Title of the book this card came from:

_____

LearningExpress books are also available in the test prep/study guide section of your local bookstore.

LEARNINGEXPRESS
20 Academy Street
P.O. Box 7100
Norwalk, CT 06852-9879

BUSINESS REPLY MAIL
FIRST CLASS MAIL PERMIT NO. 150 NORWALK, CT

POSTAGE TO BE PAID BY THE ADDRESSEE

NO POSTAGE
NECESSARY
IF MAILED
IN THE
UNITED STATES

LEARNINGEXPRESS

The new leader in test preparation and career guidance!

LearningExpress is an affiliate of Random House, Inc.

Directory of Healthcare Programs

Medix Schools
2480 Windy Hill Rd.
Marietta 30067
770-980-0002

Savannah Technical Institute
5717 White Bluff Rd.
Savannah 31405-5594
912-352-4362

Thomas Technical Institute
15689 US Hwy. 19 N
Thomasville 31792
912-225-4097

Valdosta Technical Institute
4089 Valtech Rd.
Valdosta 31602-9796
912-333-2100

HAWAII
Medical Assistant School of Hawaii, Inc.
1149 Bethel
Honolulu 96813
808-524-3363

IDAHO
America Institute of Health Technology, Inc.
6600 Emerald
Boise 83704
208-377-8080

Ricks College
Rexburg 83460-4107
208-356-1020

College of Southern Idaho
P.O. Box 1238
Twin Falls 83301
208-733-9554

ILLINOIS
Bryman College
17 North State Rd.
Chicago 60602
312-368-4911

Robert Morris College
180 No. LaSalle St.
Chicago 60601
312-836-4888

INDIANA
Indiana Vocational Technical College–Southwest
3501 First Ave.
Evansville 47710
812-426-2865

Indiana Vocational Technical College–North Central
3800 North Anthony Blvd.
Fort Wayne 46805
219-482-9171

International Business College
3811 Illinois Rd.
Fort Wayne 46804
219-432-8702

Professional Career Institute
2611 Waterfront Pkwy., East Dr.
Indianapolis 46214-2028
317-299-6001

Davenport College–Nashville
8200 Georgia St.
Merrillville 46410
219-769-5556

Indiana Vocational Technical College–South Central
8204 Hwy. 311
Sellersburg 47172
812-246-3301

Michiana College
1030 East Jefferson Blvd.
South Bend 46617
219-237-0774

IOWA

Des Moines Community College
2006 Ankeny Blvd.
Ankeny 50021
515-964-6200

Kirkwood Community College
P.O. Box 2068
Cedar Rapids 52406
319-398-5411

Palmer College of Chiropractic
1000 Brady Dr.
Davenport 52803
800-722-3648

Spencer School of Business
217 West Fifth St., P.O. Box 5065
Spencer 51301
712-262-7290

KANSAS

Topeka Technical College
1620 Northwest Gage
Topeka 66618
913-232-5858

Bryan Institute
1004 South Oliver
Wichita 67218
316-685-2284

KENTUCKY

Careercom Junior College of Business
1102 South Virginia St.
Hopkinsville 42248
502-886-1302

Kentucky College of Business
628 East Main St.
Lexington 40508
606-253-0621

Spencerian College
4627 Dixie Hwy.
Louisville 40216
502-447-1000

Owensboro Junior College of Business
1515 East 18th St., P.O. Box 1350
Owensboro 42303
502-926-4040

LOUISIANA

Commercial College of Baton Rouge
5677 Florida Blvd.
Baton Rouge 70806
504-927-3470

Domestic Health Care Institute
4826 Jamestown Ave.
Baton Rouge 70808
504-925-5312

Coastal College–Hammond
119 Yokum Rd.
Hammond 70403
504-345-3200

Coastal College–Houma
2318 West Park Ave.
Houma 70364
504-872-2800

Delta Schools, Inc.
4549 Johnston St.
Lafayette 70503
318-988-2211

Southern Technical College
303 Rue Louis XIV
Lafayette 70062
318-981-4010

Eastern College of Health Vocations
3540 I-10 Service Rd. S
Metairie 70001
504-834-8644

Delta Schools, Inc.
413 West Admiral Doyle
New Iberia 70560
318-365-7348

Directory of Healthcare Programs

Cameron College
2740 Canal St.
New Orleans 70119
504-821-5881

Coastal College
2001 Canal St.
New Orleans 70119
504-522-2400

Bryman College
2322 Canal St.
New Orleans 70119
504-822-4500

Ayers Institute, Inc.
2924 Knight St.
Shreveport 71105
318-221-1853

Commercial College
2640 Youree Dr.
Shreveport 71104
318-869-4888

Coastal College–Slidell
320 Howze Beach Rd.
Slidell 70481
504-641-2121

MAINE
Mid-State College
88 East Hardscrabble Rd.
Auburn 04210
207-783-1478

Beal College
629 Main St.
Bangor 04401
207-947-4591

Andover College
901 Washington Ave.
Portland 04103
207-774-6126

MARYLAND
Essex Community College
7201 Rossville Blvd.
Baltimore 21237
410-780-6363

Medix Schools
1017 York Rd.
Towson 21204-9840
410-337-5155

MASSACHUSETTS
Bunker Hill Community College
New Rutherford Ave.
Boston 02116
617-228-2027

Fisher College
118 Beacon St.
Boston 02116
617-236-8800

Bryman College
323 Boylston St.
Brookline 02146
617-232-6035

Aquinas College at Newton
15 Walnut Park
Newton 02158
617-969-4400

The Salter School
456 Bridge St.
Springfield 01103
413-731-7353

Associated Technical Institute
345 West Cummings Park
Woburn 01801
617-935-3838

The Salter School
155 Ararat St.
Worcester 01606
508-853-1074

MICHIGAN

Ross Technical Institute
4703 Washtenaw
Ann Arbor 48108-1411
313-434-7320

Ross Technical Institute
5757 Whitmore Lake Rd.
Brighton 48116
313-227-0160

Ross Business Institute
37065 South Gratiot
Clinton Township 48036
810-954-3083

Detroit Business Institute
1249 Washington Blvd.
Detroit 48226
313-962-6534

Bryman College
4244 Oakman Blvd.
Detroit 48204
313-834-1400

Payne-Pullman School of Trade and Commerce, Inc.
2345 Cass Ave.
Detroit 48201
313-963-4710

Ross Technical Institute
1553 Woodward
Detroit 48226
313-965-7451

Ross Medical Education Center
1036 Gilbert St.
Flint 48532
810-230-1100

Grand Rapids Educational Center
1750 Woodworth NE
Grand Rapids 49505
616-364-8464

Ross Medical Education Center
2035 28th St. SE
Grand Rapids 49508
616-243-3070

Ross Medical Education Center
1188 North West Ave.
Jackson 49202
517-782-7677

Grand Rapids Educational Center
5349 West Main
Kalamazoo 49009
616-381-9616

Lansing Community College
419 North Capitol Ave.
Lansing 48901-7210
517-483-9850

Ross Medical Education Center
913 West Holmes
Lansing 48910
517-887-0180

National Education Center–National Institute of Technology
18000 Newburgh Rd.
Livonia 48152
313-464-7387

Schoolcraft College
18600 Haggerty Rd.
Livonia 48152
313-462-4400

Ross Business Institute
1285 North Telegraph
Monroe 48161
313-243-5456

Professional Careers Institute
23300 Greenfield Ave.
Oak Park 48237
810-967-2500

Directory of Healthcare Programs

Ross Technical Institute
20820 Greenfield Rd.
Oak Park 48237
313-967-3100

Pontiac Business Institute–Oxford
775 West Drahner Rd.
Oxford 48237
313-628-4846

Detroit Business Educational Center
19100 Fort St.
Riverview 48192
313-479-0660

Ross Business Institute
22293 Eureka
Taylor 48180
313-563-0640

Carnegie Institute
550 Stephenson Hwy.
Troy 48083
810-589-1078

Delta College
University Center 48710
517-686-9000

Macomb Community College
14500 Twelve Mile Rd.
Warren 48093-3896
810-445-7999

Ross Medical Education Center
950 Norton Ave., Park Row Mall
Roosevelt Park 49441
616-739-1531

Ross Medical Education Center
4054 Bay Rd.
Saginaw 48603
517-793-9800

Ross Medical Education Center
26417 Hoover Rd.
Warren 48089
810-758-7200

Ross Medical Education Center
253 Summit Dr.
Pontiac 48053
313-683-1166

National Education Center–National
Institute of Technology
2620 Remico St. SW
Wyoming 40509
616-538-3170

MINNESOTA
Medical Institute of Minnesota
5503 Green Valley Dr.
Bloomington 55437
612-844-0064

Duluth Business University, Inc.
412 West Superior St.
Duluth 55802
218-722-3361

Northwest Technical College–East
Grand Forks
Hwy. 220 N
East Grand Forks 56721
218-773-3441

Concorde Career Institute
12 North 12th St.
Minneapolis 55403
612-341-3850

Globe College of Business
175 Fifth St., P.O. Box 60
Saint Paul 55101-2901
612-224-4378

Lakeland Medical and Dental Academy
1402 West Lake St.
Minneapolis 55408
612-827-5656

Rochester Community College
851 30th Ave. SE
Rochester 55904-4999
507-285-7210

MISSOURI

Bryan Institute
12184 Natural Bridge Rd.
Bridgeton 63044
314-291-0241

Metro Business College of Cape Girardeau
1732 North Kingshighway
Cape Girardeau 63701
314-334-9181

Metro Business College
1407 Southwest Blvd.
Jefferson City 65109
314-635-6600

Concorde Career Institute
3239 Broadway
Kansas City 64111
816-531-5223

Tad Technical Institute
7910 Troost Ave.
Kansas City 64131
816-361-5640

Midwest Institute for Medical Assistants
112 West Jefferson
Kirkwood 63122
314-965-8363

Metro Business College
1202 E. Hwy 72
Rolla 65401
314-364-8464

Al-Med Academy
10963 Saint Charles Rock Rd.
Saint Louis 63074
314-739-4450

Missouri School for Doctors' Assistants
10121 Manchester Rd.
Saint Louis 63122
314-821-7700

Saint Louis College of Health Careers
4484 West Pine
Saint Louis 63108
314-652-0300

Phillips Junior College
1010 West Sunshine
Springfield 65807
417-864-7220

NEBRASKA

Southeast Community College–Lincoln Campus
8800 O St.
Lincoln 68520
402-471-3333

Institute of Computer Science
808 South 74th Place, 7400 Court Building
Omaha 68114
402-393-7064

Omaha College of Health Careers
10845 Harney St.
Omaha 68154
402-333-1400

NEVADA

Academy for Career Education
3120 East Desert Inn Rd.
Las Vegas 89121
702-732-7748

Canterbury Career Schools
2215C Renaissance Dr.
Las Vegas 89119
702-798-6929

NEW HAMPSHIRE

New Hampshire Technical College at Claremont
One College Dr.
Claremont 03743
603-542-7744

Directory of Healthcare Programs

NEW JERSEY
Omega Institute
Rte. 130 S. Cinnaminson Mall
Cinnaminson 08077
609-786-2200

Star Technical Institute–Deptford
251 Delsea Dr.
Deptford 08104
609-384-2888

Dover Business College
15 East Blackwell St.
Dover 07801
201-366-6700

Barclay Career School
28 South Harrison St.
East Orange 07017
201-673-0500

Star Technical Institute
2224 U.S. Hwy. 130, Park Plaza
Edgewater Park 08010
609-877-2727

Drake College of Business
Nine Caldwell Place
Elizabeth 07201
201-352-5509

American Business Academy
66 Moore St.
Hackensack 07601
201-488-9400

Star Technical Institute
1255 Rte. 70
Lakewood 08701
908-901-9710

Star Technical Institute–Oakhurst
2105 Hwy. 35
Oakhurst 07755
908-493-1660

Business Training Institute
Four Forest Ave.
Paramus 07652
201-845-9300

Ho-Ho-Kus School
27 South Franklin Tpke.
Ramsey 07446
201-327-8877

Berdan Institute
265 Rte. 46
Totowa 07512
201-256-3444

NEW MEXICO
Franklin Medical College–Branch Campus
2400 Louisiana Blvd. NE
Albuquerque 87110
505-883-4800

Pima Medical Institute
2201 San Pedro NE
Albuquerque 87110
505-881-1234

NEW YORK
Bryant and Stratton Business Institute–Buffalo
1028 Main St.
Buffalo 14202
716-884-9120

Suburban Technical School
2650 Sunrise Hwy.
East Islip 11730
516-224-5001

New York School for Medical and Dental Assistants
116-16 Queens Blvd.
Forest Hills 11375
718-793-2330

Suburban Technical School
175 Fulton Ave.
Hempstead 11550
516-481-6660

Blake Business School–New York City
20 Cooper Square
New York 10003
212-254-1233

Mandl School
254 West 54th St.
New York 10019
212-247-3434

Bayley Seton Hospital School Physicians Assistant
75 Vanderbilt Ave.
Staten Island 10304
718-390-6000

Hudson Valley Community College
80 Vandenburgh Ave.
Troy 12180
518-283-1100

NORTH CAROLINA
Central Piedmont Community College
P.O. Box 35009
Charlotte 28235
704-342-6633

Pitt Community College
P.O. Drawer 7007
Greenville 27835
919-321-4200

Miller-Motte Business College
606 South College Rd.
Wilmington 28403
910-392-4660

NORTH DAKOTA
Interstate Business College
520 East Main Ave.
Bismarck 58501
701-255-0779

Interstate Business College
2720 32nd Ave. SW
Fargo 58103
701-232-2477

OHIO
Akron Medical-Dental Institute
733 West Marker St.
Akron 44303
216-762-9788

Mahoning County Joint Vocational School District
7300 North Palmyra Rd.
Canfield 44406
216-533-3923

Fairfield Career Center
4000 Columbus Lancaster Rd.
Carroll 43112
614-836-4541

RETS Technical Center
116 Westpark Rd.
Centerville 45459
513-433-3410

Institute of Medical-Dental Technology
4452 Eastgate Blvd.
Cincinnati 45246
513-753-5030

Institute of Medical-Dental Technology
375 Glensprings Dr.
Cincinnati 45246
513-851-8500

Cleveland Institute of Dental-Medical Assistants
1836 Euclid Ave.
Cleveland 44115
216-241-2930

Cuyahoga Community College District
700 Carnegie Ave.
Cleveland 44115-2878
216-987-6000

Directory of Healthcare Programs

MTI Business College
1140 Euclid Ave
Cleveland 44115-1603
216-621-8228

National Education Center
14445 Broadway Ave.
Cleveland 44125
216-475-7520

Sawyer College of Business
3150 Mayfield Rd.
Cleveland Heights 44118
216-932-0911

American School of Technology
2100 Morse Rd.
Columbus 43229
614-436-4820

Columbus Para Professional Institute
1077 Lexington Ave.
Columbus 43201
614-299-0200

Technology Education Center
288 South Hamilton Rd.
Columbus 43213
614-759-7700

National Education Center–National Institute of Technology
1225 Orlen Ave.
Cuyahoga Falls 44221
216-923-9959

Southwestern College of Business
225 West First St.
Dayton 48402
513-294-2103

Warren County Career Center
3525 N SR 48
Lebanon 45036-1099
513-932-5677

ESI Career Center
1985 North Ridge Rd. E
Lorain 44055
216-277-8832

Cleveland Institute of Dental-Medical Assistants
5733 Hopkins Rd.
Mentor 44060
216-946-9530

Knox County Career Center
306 Martinsburg Rd.
Mount Vernon 43050
614-397-5820

Tri-County Vocational School
15675 SR 691
Nelsonville 45764
614-753-3511

Boheckers Business College
326 East Main St.
Ravenna 44266
330-297-7319

Belmont Technical College
120 Fox Shannon Place
Saint Clairsville 43950
614-695-9500

Institute of Medical-Dental Professional Skills Institute
1232 Flaire Dr.
Toledo 43615
419-531-9610

Stautzenberger College
5355 Southwyck Blvd.
Toledo 43614
419-866-5167

University of Toledo
2801 West Bancroft
Toledo 43606
419-537-2072

Trumbull County Joint Vocational School District
528 Educational Hwy.
Warren 44483
216-847-0503

OKLAHOMA
Southern Oklahoma Area Vocational-Technical Center
2610 Sam Noble Pkwy.
Ardmore 73401
405-223-2070

Platt College
6125 West Reno
Oklahoma City 73127
405-789-5052

De Marge College
3608 Northwest 58th
Oklahoma City 73112
405-947-1425

Francis Tuttle Area Vocational-Technical Center
12777 North Rockwell Ave.
Oklahoma City 73142-2789
405-722-7799

Wright Business School
2219 Southwest 74th St.
Oklahoma City 73159
405-681-2300

Central Oklahoma Area Vocational Technical School
1720 South Main
Sapulpa 74030
918-224-9300

Bryan Institute
2843 East 51st St.
Tulsa 74105-1709
918-749-6891

OREGON
Apollo College-Portland, Inc.
2600 Southeast 98th Ave.
Portland 97266
503-761-6100

College of America
921 Southwest Washington
Portland 97205
503-242-9000

Western Business College
425 Southwest Sixth Ave.
Portland 97204
503-222-3225

Pioneer Pacific College
25195 Southwest Parkway Ave.
Wilsonville 97070
503-682-3903

PENNSYLVANIA
Altoona Area Vocational Technology School
1500 Fourth Ave.
Altoona 16602
814-946-8490

Allied Medical Centers, Inc.
104 Woodward Rd.
Edwardsville 18704
717-288-8400

J. H. Thompson Academies
2910 State Rd.
Erie 16508
814-456-6217

Academy of Medical Arts and Business
279 Boas St.
Harrisburg 17102
717-233-2172

Directory of Healthcare Programs

National Education Center–Thompson Institute Campus
5650 Derry St.
Harrisburg 17111
717-564-4112

Star Technical Institute–Kingston
212 Wyoming Ave.
Kingston 18704
717-829-6960

Career Training Academy
244 Center Rd.
Monroeville 15146
412-372-3900

Career Training Academy
703 Fifth Ave.
New Kensington 15068
412-337-1000

The Craft Institute
27 South 12th St.
Philadelphia 19107
215-592-4600

Delaware Valley Academy of Medical and Dental Assistants
3330 Grant Ave.
Philadelphia 19114
215-676-1200

National Education Center
3440 Marker St.
Philadelphia 19104
215-387-1530

Duffs Business Institute
110 Ninth St.
Pittsburgh 15222
412-261-4520

ICM School of Business
10-14 Wood St.
Pittsburgh 15222
412-261-2647

Median School of Allied Health Careers
125 Seventh St.
Pittsburgh 15222-3400
800-570-0693

North Hills School of Health Occupations
1500 Northway Mall
Pittsburgh 15237
412-367-8003

Sawyer School
717 Liberty Ave.
Pittsburgh 15222
412-261-5700

Antonelli Medical and Professional Institute
1700 Industrial Pkwy.
Pottstown 19464
610-323-7270

Allied Medical Careers, Inc.
2901 Pittston Ave.
Scranton 18505
717-342-8000

Star Technical Institute–Whitehall
1541 Alta Dr.
Whitehall 18052
215-434-9963

Berks Technical Institute
832 North Park Rd., Four Park Plaza
Wyomissing 19610
215-372-1722

SOUTH CAROLINA
Trident Technical College
P.O. Box 118067
Charleston 29423-8067
803-572-6111

Central Carolina Technical College
506 North Guignard Dr.
Sumter 29150
803-778-1961

TENNESSEE

Draughon College
3200 Elvis Presley Blvd.
Memphis 38116
901-332-7800

Davidson Technical College
212 Pavillion Blvd.
Nashville 37217-1002
615-360-3300

Fugazzi College
5042 Linbar Dr.
Nashville 37217
615-333-3344

Medical Career College
537 Main St.
Nashville 37206
901-644-7365

TEXAS

Bryan Institute
1719 Pioneer Pkwy. W
Arlington 76013
817-265-5588

Southern Career Institute, Inc.
2301 South Congress
Austin 78704
512-326-1415

ATI Health Education Center
8150 Brookriver Dr.
Dallas 75247
214-637-0980

PCI Health Training Center
8101 John Carpenter Fwy.
Dallas 75247
214-263-8724

Career Centers of Texas El Paso, Inc.
8375 Brunham Dr.
El Paso 79907
915-595-1935

Western Technical Institute
4710 Alabama St., P.O. Box M
El Paso 79951
915-566-9621

ATI Health Education Center
1200 Summit Ave.
Fort Worth 76102
817-429-1045

Avalon Vocational Technical Institute
1407 Texas St.
Fort Worth 765102
817-877-5511

The Academy of Health Care Professions
1919 North Loop W
Houston 77008
713-741-2633

Bradford School of Business
4669 Southwest Hwy.
Houston 77027
713-629-8940

International Career School
7647 Belfort
Houston 77061
713-649-0067

Bryman College
9724 Beechnut
Houston 77036
713-776-3656

Bryman College
16416 North Chase Dr.
Houston 77060
713-447-6656

Southern Careers Institute–South Texas
3233 North 38th
McAllen 78501
210-687-1415

Directory of Healthcare Programs

Avalon Vocational Technical Institute
4241 Tanglewood
Odessa 79762
915-367-2622

San Antonio College of Medical and
Dental Assistants–South
3900 North 23rd
McAllen 78501
210-630-1499

National Education Center–NIT Campus
3622 Fredericksburg Rd.
San Antonio 78201
210-733-6000

San Antonio College of Medical and
Dental Assistants–Central
4205 San Pedro Ave.
San Antonio 78212
210-733-0777

San Antonio College of Medical and
Dental Assistants
5280 Medical Dr.
San Antonio 78229
210-692-0241

Southwest School of Business and
Technical Careers
602 West South Cross
San Antonio 78221
512-921-0951

Southwest School of Medical Assistants
201 West Sheridan
San Antonio 78204
512-224-2296

UTAH
Stevens-Henager College of Business
2168 Washington Blvd.
Ogden 84401
801-394-7791

American Institute of Medical-Dental
Technology
1675 North 200 West
Provo 84604
801-377-2900

Stevens-Henager College of Business
25 East 1700 South
Provo 84606-6157
801-375-5455

Bryman School
1144 West 3300 South
Salt Lake City 84119-3330
801-975-7000

VIRGINIA
Career Development Center
605 Thimble Shoals
Newport News 23606
804-599-4088

Commonwealth College
300 Boush St.
Norfolk 23510
804-625-5891

National Education Center–Kee
Business College Campus
861 Glenrock Rd.
Norfolk 23418
804-461-2922

Tidewater Technical
1760 East Little Creek Rd.
Norfolk 23518
804-588-2121

National Education Center–Kee
Business College Campus
6301 Midlothian Tpke.
Richmond 23225
804-745-3300

Dominion Business School
4142-1 Melrose Ave.
Roanoke 24017
703-362-7738

Commonwealth College
4160 Virginia Beach Blvd.
Virginia Beach 23452
804-340-0222

Tidewater Technical
2697 Dean Dr.
Virginia Beach 23452
804-340-2121

WASHINGTON
Eton Technical Institute
209 East Casino Rd.
Everett 98204
206-353-4888

Eton Technical Institute
31919 Sixth Ave. S
Federal Way 98063
206-941-5800

Eton Technical Institute
3649 Frontage Rd.
Port Orchard 98366
206-479-3866

Pima Medical Institute
1627 Eastlake Ave. E
Seattle 98102
206-322-6100

Seattle Vocational Institute
315 22nd Ave. S
Seattle 98144
206-587-4950

Spokane Community College
North 1810 Greene Ave.
Spokane 99201
509-536-7000

Trend College
North 214 Wall St.
Spokane 99201
509-838-3521

WEST VIRGINIA
Boone County Career & Technical Center
P.O. Box 50B
Danville 25053
304-369-4585

Huntington Junior College
900 Fifth Ave.
Huntington 25701
304-697-7550

Opportunities Industrialization Center–North Central West Virginia
120 Jackson St.
Fairmont 26554
304-366-8142

West Virginia Career College
148 Willey St.
Morgantown 26505
304-296-8282

WISCONSIN
Northeast Wisconsin Technical College
2740 West Mason St., P.O. Box 19042
Green Bay 54307-9042
414-498-5400

Blackhawk Technical College
P.O. Box 5009
Janesville 53547
608-756-4121

Madison Area Technical College
3550 Anderson St.
Madison 53704
608-246-6100

Directory of Healthcare Programs

Milwaukee Area Technical College
700 West State St.
Milwaukee 53233
414-297-6600

Waukesha County Technical College
800 Main St.
Pewaukee 53072
414-691-5566

Wisconsin Indianhead Technical College
505 Pine Ridge Dr., P.O. Box 10B
Shell Lake 54871
715-468-2815

Mid-State Technical College-Main Campus
500 32nd St. N
Wisconsin Rapids 54494
715-423-5650

NURSE ASSISTANT
ALABAMA
Read State Technical College
P.O. Box 588
Evergreen 36401
205-578-1313

Trenholm State Technical College
1225 Air Base Blvd.
Montgomery 36108
334-832-9000

Bevill State Community College
P.O. Box Drawer K
Sumiton 35148
205-648-3271

ARIZONA
Gateway Community College
108 North 40th St.
Phoenix 80534
602-392-5000

Eastern Arizona College
600 Church St.
Thatcher 85552-0769
602-428-8322

Pima Community College
2202 West Anklam Rd.
Tucson 85709-0001
520-206-6640

Pima Medical College
3350 East Grant Rd.
Tucson 85716
520-326-1600

Tucson College
7302-10 East 22nd St.
Tucson 85710
520-296-3261

ARKANSAS
Gateway Technical College
P.O. Box 3350
Batesville 72503
501-793-7581

Crowley's Ridge Technical School
P.O. Box 925
Forrest City 72335
501-633-5411

Eastern College of Health Vocation
6423 Forbing Rd.
Little Rock 72209
501-568-0211

Great Rivers Vocational-Technical School
P.O. Box 747
McGehee 71654
501-222-5360

Arkansas Valley Technical Institute
Hwy. 23 N, P.O. Box 4506
Ozark 72949
501-667-2117

Black River Technical College
Hwy. 304, P.O. Box 468
Pocahontas 72455
501-892-4565

CALIFORNIA
American School of X-Ray
13723 Harvard Place
Gardena 90249
213-770-4001

Hacienda La Puente Unified School
District–Valley Vocational Center
15959 East Gale Ave.
La Puente 91749
818-968-4638

Educorp Career College
230 East Third St.
Long Beach 90802
213-437-0501

Allied Nursing Center, Inc.
3806 Beverly Blvd.
Los Angeles 90064
213-389-9337

Nova Institute of Health Technology
520 North Euclid Ave.
Ontario 91762
909-984-5027

Butte College
3536 Butte Campus Dr.
Oroville 95965
916-895-2511

Mission College
3000 Mission College Blvd.
Santa Clara 95054-1897
408-748-2700

Allan Hancock College
800 South College Dr.
Santa Maria 93454
805-922-6966

Santa Rosa Junior College
1501 Mendocino Ave.
Santa Rosa 95401-4395
707-527-4100

Simi Valley Adult School
3192 Los Angeles Ave.
Simi Valley 93065
805-527-4840

COLORADO
San Luis Valley Area Vocational School
1011 Main St.
Alamosa 81101
719-589-5871

Colorado Mountain College
P.O. Box 10001
Glenwood Springs 81620
970-945-7481

PPI Health Careers School
2345 North Academy Blvd.
Colorado Springs 80909
719-596-7400

CONNECTICUT
Connecticut Business Institute
809 Main St.
East Hartford 06108
203-291-2880

Connecticut Business Institute
605 Broad St.
Stratford 06497
203-377-1775

FLORIDA
Atlantic Vocational Technical Center
4700 Coconut Creek Pkwy.
Coconut Creek 33063
954-977-2000

Directory of Healthcare Programs

Brevard Community College
1519 Clearlake Rd.
Fort Lauderdale 33304
407-632-1111

Beacon Career Institute, Inc.
2900 Northwest 183rd St.
Miami 33056
305-620-4637

Nurse Assistant Training School, Inc.
5154 Okeechobee Blvd.
West Palm Beach 33417
561-683-1400

MASSACHUSETTS
Assabet Valley Regional Vocational Technical School
215 Fitchburg St.
Marlborough 01752
508-485-9430

MICHIGAN
Ross Medical Education Center
1036 Gilbert St.
Flint 48532
810-230-1100

Detroit Business Institute
1249 Washington Blvd.
Detroit 48226
313-962-6534

Ross Technical Institute
1553 Woodward
Detroit 48226
313-371-2131

Ross Medical Education Center
15670 East Eight Mile Rd.
Detroit 48205

Ross Technical Institute
20820 Greenfield Rd.
Oak Park 48237
313-967-3100

Ross Medical Education Center
950 Norton Ave., Park Row Mall
Roosevelt Park 49441
616-739-1531

Ross Medical Education Center
4054 Bay Rd.
Saginaw 46803
517-793-9800

MINNESOTA
Duluth Technical College
2101 Trinity Rd.
Duluth 55811
218-722-2801

Itasca Community College
1851 Hwy. 169 E
Grand Rapids 55744
218-327-4460

Northeast Metro Technical College
3300 Century Ave. N
White Bear Lake 55110
612-770-2351

MISSISSIPPI
Northwest Mississippi Community College
Hwy. 51 N
Senatobia 38668
601-562-5262

MISSOURI
Cape Girardeau Area Vocational-Technical School
301 North Clarke Ave.
Cape Girardeau 63701
314-334-3358

Saint Louis College of Health Careers
4484 West Pine
Saint Louis 63108
314-652-0300

75

Sikeston Area Vocational Technical School
1002 Virginia
Sikeston 63801
314-472-2581

MONTANA
Dawson Community College
300 College Dr.
Glendive 59330
406-365-3396

Great Falls Vocational Technical Center
2100 16th Ave. S
Great Falls 59405
406-791-2100

NEBRASKA
Opportunity Industrialization Center Omaha
2724 North 24th St.
Omaha 68111
402-457-4222

NEW MEXICO
Albuquerque Technical-Vocational Institute
525 Buena Vista SE
Albuquerque 87106
505-224-3000

Franklin Medical College–Branch Campus
2400 Louisiana Blvd. NE
Albuquerque 87110
505-883-4800

Crownpoint Institute of Technology
P.O. Box 849
Crownpoint 87313
505-786-5851

NEW YORK
CM First Step Training Center
1360 Fulton St.
Brooklyn 11242
718-783-5656

Municipal Training Center
44 Court St.
Brooklyn 11201
718-855-4144

A Business Career Institute, Inc.
91-31 Queens Blvd.
Elmhurst 11373
718-458-1500

Suburban Technical School
175 Fulton Ave.
Hempstead 11550
516-481-6660

Silhouette
3187 Steinway St.
Long Island City 11103
718-777-1380

Cashier Training Institute
500 Eighth Ave.
New York 10018
212-564-0500

New York Training Institute for NLP
145 Ave. of the Americas
New York 10012
212-647-1600

Superior Career Institute, Inc.
116 West 14th St.
New York 10038
212-675-2140

Travel Institute
15 Park Row
New York 10038
212-349-3331

Directory of Healthcare Programs

NORTH CAROLINA
Roanoke-Chowan Community College
Rte. 2, P.O. Box 46A
Ahoeskie 27910
919-332-5921

Coastal Carolina Community College
444 Western Blvd.
Jacksonville 28546-6877
910-938-6246

Robeson Community College
P.O. Box 1420
Lumberton 28359
910-738-7101

Craven Community College
800 College Court.
New Bern 28562
919-638-4131

Piedmont Community College
P.O. Box 1197
Roxboro 27573
910-599-1181

Brunswick Community College
P.O. Box 30
Supply 28461
910-754-6900

NORTH DAKOTA
Meyer Vocational Technical School
2045 Northwest Third, P.O. Box 2126
Minot 58702
701-852-0427

OHIO
Madison Local Schools-Madison Adult Education
600 Esley Ln.
Mansfield 44905
419-589-6363

Tri-Rivers Career Center
2222 Marion Mount Gilead Rd.
Marion 43302
614-389-6347

Gallia Jackson Vinton JUSD
P.O. Box 157
Rio Grande 45674
614-245-5334

OKLAHOMA
Southwest Area Vocational-Technical Center
1121 North Spurgeon
Altus 73521
405-477-2250

Mid-Del College
3420 South Sunnylane
Del City 73115
405-677-8311

Tulsa County Area Vocational-Technical School District 18
3802 North Peoria
Tulsa 74106
918-428-2261

OREGON
Southwestern Oregon Community College
1988 Newmark Ave.
Coos Bay 97420
541-888-7339

PENNSYLVANIA
Delaware County Institute of Training
615 Ave. of the States
Chester 19013
610-874-1888

Allied Medical Careers, Inc.
104 Woodward Hill Rd.
Edwardsville 18704
717-288-8400

Pennsylvania State University-Allentown Campus
6090 Mohr Ln.
Fogelsville 18051-9733
610-821-6577

McKeesport Hospital School of Nursing Assistants
1500 Fifth Ave.
McKeesport 15132
412-664-2139

American Institute of Design
1616 Orthodox St.
Philadelphia 19124
215-288-8200

Antonelli Medical and Professional Institute
1700 Industrial Hwy.
Pottstown 19664
610-323-7270

Presbyterian Home Nurse Assistant School
P.O. Box 551
Phillipsburg 16866
814-342-6090

Allied Medical Careers, Inc.
2901 Pittston Ave.
Scranton 18505
717-288-8400

Advanced Career Training
Southwest Corner 69th & Markey
Upper Darby 19505
610-352-3600

SOUTH CAROLINA
Chris Logan Career College
1125 15-401 Bypass
Bennettsville 29512
803-479-4076

Chris Logan Career College
P.O. Box 261
Myrtle Beach 29578-0261
803-448-6302

Chris Logan Career College
256 South Pike Rd.
Sumter 29150
803-775-2667

Trident Technical College
P.O. Box 118067
Charleston 29423-8067
803-572-6215

TENNESSEE
Elizabethton State Area Vocational Technical School
1500 Arney St., P.O. Box 789
Elizabethton 37643
615-542-4174

Hohenwald State Area Vocational-Technical School
813 West Main
Hohenwald 38462-2201
615-796-5822

Knoxville State Area Vocational-Technical School
1100 Liberty St.
Knoxville 37919
615-546-5568

Rice College
1515 Magnolia Ave., NE
Knoxville 37917
615-637-9899

Draughons College
3200 Elvis Presley Blvd.
Memphis 38116
901-332-7800

Directory of Healthcare Programs

Memphis Area Vocational-Technical School
550 Alabama Ave.
Memphis 38105-3799
901-543-6100

Rice College
1399 Madison Ave.
Memphis 38104
901-725-1000

Davidson Technical College
212 Pavilion Blvd.
Nashville 37217-1002
615-360-3300

Medical Career College
537 Main St.
Nashville 37206
615-255-7531

Paris State Area Vocational-Technical School
312 South Wilson St.
Paris 38242
901-644-7365

TEXAS
Delta Career Institute
1310 Pennsylvania Ave.
Beaumont 77701
409-833-6161

Brazos Business College
1702 South Texas Ave.
Bryan 77802
409-822-6423

Southwest School of Business and Technical Careers
272 Commercial St.
Eagle Pass 78852
512-773-1373

Texas State Technical College–Harlingen Campus
2424 Boxwood
Harlingen 78550-3697
210-425-0600

Houston Medical Career Training, Inc.
2420 Garland Dr.
Houston 77087
713-641-6300

Transworld Academy, Inc.
6220 West Park
Houston 77057
713-266-6594

Southern Careers Institute–South Texas
3233 North 38th
McAllen 78501
210-687-1415

Chenier
2819 Loop 306
San Angelo 76904
915-944-4404

Southwest School of Business and Technical Careers
602 West South Cross
San Antonio 78221
210-921-0951

UTAH
Bridgerland Applied Technology Center
1301 North 600 West
Logan 84321
801-753-6780

Salt Lake Community College–Skills Center
South City Campus, 1575 South State St.
Salt Lake City 84115
801-957-3354

VIRGINIA

Southside Training Skill Center
Nottoway County
P.O. Box 258
Crewe 23930
804-645-7471

Career Development Center
605 Thimble Shoals
Newport News 23606
804-599-4088

Tidewater Technical
616 Denbigh Blvd.
Newport News 23602
804-874-2121

Tidewater Technical
1760 East Little Creek Rd.
Norfolk 23518
804-588-2121

Blue Ridge Nursing Home School
Commerce St., P.O. Box 459
Stuart 24171
703-694-7161

Tidewater Technical
2697 Dean Dr.
Virginia Beach 23452
804-340-2121

WASHINGTON

Lower Columbia College
P.O. Box 3010
Longview 98632
206-577-2300

Big Bend Community College
7662 Chanute
Moses Lake 98837
509-762-5351

Bates Technical College
1101 South Yakima Ave.
Tacoma 98405
206-596-1500

Yakima Valley Community College
P.O. Box 1647
Yakima 98907
509-574-4712

WISCONSIN

Fox Valley Technical College
1825 North Bluemound Dr.
Appleton 54913-2277
414-735-5600

Lakeshore Vocational Training and Adult
Education System District
1290 North Ave.
Cleveland 53015
414-458-4183

Southwest Wisconsin Technical College
Hwy. 18 E
Fennimore 53809
608-822-3262

Wisconsin Area Vocational Training and
Adult Education System–Moraine Park
235 North National Ave., P.O. Box 1940
Fond Du Lac 54936-1940
414-922-8611

Northwest Wisconsin Technical College
2740 West Mason St., P.O. Box 19042
Green Bay 54307-9042
414-498-5400

Blackhawk Technical College
P.O. Box 5009
Janesville 53547
608-756-4121

Gateway Technical College
3520 30th Ave.
Kenosha 53144-1690
414-656-6900

Western Wisconsin Technical College
304 North Sixth St., P.O. Box 908
La Crosse 54602-0908
608-785-9200

Directory of Healthcare Programs

Madison Area Technical College
3550 Anderson St.
Madison 53704
608-246-6100

Milwaukee Area Technical College
700 West State St.
Milwaukee 53233
414-297-6600

Waukesha County Technical College
800 Main St.
Pewaukee 53072
414-691-5566

Nicolet Vocational Training and Adult Education System District
P.O. Box 518
Rhinelander 54501
715-365-4410

Wisconsin Indianhead Technical College
505 Pine Ridge Dr., P.O. Box 108
Shell Lake 54871
715-468-2815

North Central Technical College
1000 Campus Dr.
Wausau 54401-1899
715-675-3331

Mid-State Technical College-Main Campus
500 32nd St. N
Wisconsin Rapids 54494
715-423-5650

PHYSICAL THERAPY ASSISTANT TECHNOLOGY

ALABAMA
University of Alabama at Birmingham
UAB MJH 107 2010
Birmingham 35294-2010
205-934-3443

George C. Wallace State Community College–Hanceville
801 Main St. NW, P.O. Box 2000
Hanceville 35077-2000
205-352-6403

Community College of the Air Force
Maxwell Air Force Base
Montgomery 36112
334-953-6436

ARIZONA
Long Medical Institute
4126 North Black Canyon Hwy.
Phoenix 85017
602-279-9333

Pima Medical Institute
2300 East Broadway Rd.
Tempe 85282
602-345-7777

ARKANSAS
University of Central Arkansas
201 Donaghey Ave.
Conway 72035-0001
501-450-5000

CALIFORNIA
De Anza College
21250 Stevens Creek Blvd.
Cupertino 95014
408-864-5678

Imperial Valley College
P.O. Box 158
Imperial 92251-0158
619-352-8320

Loma Linda University
Loma Linda 92350
909-824-4931

Cerritos College
11110 Alondra Blvd.
Norwalk 90650
310-860-2451

Sawyer College at Ventura
2101 East Gonzales Rd.
Oxnard 93030
805-485-6000

COLORADO
Aims Community College
P.O. Box 69
Greeley 80632
970-330-8008

CONNECTICUT
Manchester Community College
60 Bidwell St., P.O. Box 1045
Manchester 06040-1046
203-647-6000

FLORIDA
Broward Community College
225 East Las Olas Blvd.
Fort Lauderdale 33301
954-761-7464

Miami-Dade Community College
300 Northeast Second Ave.
Miami 33132
305-237-3336

Charlotte Vocational-Technical Center
18300 Toledo Blade Blvd.
Port Charlotte 33948-3399
941-629-6819

Saint Petersburg Junior College
P.O. Box 13489
Saint Petersburg 33733
813-341-3611

GEORGIA
Athens Area Technical Institute
800 Hwy 29 N
Athens 30601
706-542-8050

Gwinnett Technical Institute
1250 Atkinson Rd., P.O. Box 1505
Lawrenceville 30246-1505
404-962-7580

IDAHO
American Institute of Health Technology, Inc.
6600 Emerald
Boise 83704
208-377-8080

ILLINOIS
Belleville Area College
2500 Carlyle Rd.
Belleville 62221
618-235-2700

Morton College
3801 South Central Ave.
Cicero 60650
708-656-8000

KANSAS
Neosho County Community College
1000 South Allen
Chanute 66720
316-431-2820

Colby Community College
1255 South Range
Colby 67701
913-462-3984

Cloud County Community College
2221 Campus Dr., P.O. Box 1002
Concordia 66901-1002
913-243-1435

Allen County Community College
1801 North Cottonwood
Iola 66749
316-365-5116

Kansas City Area Vocational Technical School
2220 North 59th St.
Kansas City 66104
913-596-5500

KAW Area Vocational-Technical School
5724 Huntoon
Topeka 66604
913-273-7140

Directory of Healthcare Programs

North Central Kansas Area Vocational Technical School
P.O. Box 507
Beloit 67420
913-738-2276

Salina Area Vocational Technical School
2562 Scanlan Ave.
Salina 67401
913-825-2261

Wichita Area Vocational Technical School
324 No. Emporia
Wichita 67202
316-833-4370

MARYLAND
Baltimore City Community College
2901 Liberty Heights Ave.
Baltimore 21215
410-333-5555

MASSACHUSETTS
Newbury College
129 Fisher Ave.
Brookline 02146
617-730-7000

Becker College–Worcester
61 Sever St.
Worcester 01615-0071
508-791-9241

MICHIGAN
Delta College
University Center 48710
517-686-9093

Macomb Community College
14500 Twelve Mile Rd.
Warren 48093-3896
810-445-7000

MINNESOTA
Anoka-Ramsey Community College
11200 Mississippi Blvd.
Coon Rapids 55433
612-427-2600

College of Saint Catherine-Saint Mary's Campus
2500 South Sixth St.
Minneapolis 55454
612-690-7700

MISSOURI
Jefferson College
1000 Viking Dr.
Hillsboro 63050
314-789-3951

NEW JERSEY
University of Medicine and Dentistry of New Jersey
65 Bergen St.
Newark 07107
201-982-4821

NEW YORK
Genesee Community College
One College Rd.
Batavia 14020
716-343-0055

CUNY Kingsborough Community College
2001 Oriental Blvd.
Brooklyn 11235
718-368-5000

Nassau Community College
One Education Dr.
Garden City 11530
516-572-7345

CUNY La Guardia Community College
31-10 Thomson Ave.
Long Island City 11101
718-482-7200

Suffolk County Community College-
Ammerman Campus
533 College Rd.
Selden 11784
516-451-4110

NORTH CAROLINA
Central Piedmont Community College
P.O. Box 35009
Charlotte 28235
704-342-6633

OHIO
Cuyahoga Community College District
700 Carnegie Ave.
Cleveland 44115-2878
216-987-6000

Stark Technical College
6200 Frank Ave. NW
Canton 44720
216-494-6170

Kent State University–East Liverpool
Regional Campus
400 East Fourth St.
East Liverpool 43920
216-385-3805

OREGON
Mount Hood Community College
26000 Southeast Stark St.
Gresham 97030
513-667-6422

PENNSYLVANIA
Harcom Junior College
Morris and Montgomery Ave.
Bryn Mawr 19010
610-526-6086

Pennsylvania State University-Hazleton
Campus
Highacres
Hazleton 19201
717-454-8731

Community College of Allegheny
County
800 Allegheny Ave.
Pittsburgh 15233-1895
412-323-2323

Lehigh County Community College
4525 Education Park Dr.
Schnecksville 28078-2598
610-799-2121

SOUTH CAROLINA
Trident Technical College
P.O. Box 118067
Charleston 29423-8067
803-572-6111

TENNESSEE
Volunteer State Community College
1360 Nashville Pike
Gallatin 37066
615-452-8600

TEXAS
Amarillo College
P.O. Box 447
Amarillo 79178
806-354-6071

Tarrant County Junior College District
1500 Houston St.
Fort Worth 76102
817-336-7851

Houston Community College System
22 Waugh Dr., P.O. Box 7849
Houston 77270-7849
713-869-5021

Transworld Academy, Inc.
6220 West Park
Houston 77057
713-266-6594

Directory of Healthcare Programs

VIRGINIA
Northern Virginia Community College
4001 Wakefield Chapel Rd.
Annandale 22003
703-323-3129

WISCONSIN
Northeast Wisconsin Technical College
2740 West Mason St., P.O. Box 19042
Green Bay 54307-9042
414-498-5400

Milwaukee Area Technical College
700 West State St.
Milwaukee 53233
414-297-6600

RADIOLOGIC TECHNOLOGY

ALABAMA
Jefferson State Community College
2601 Carson Rd.
Birmingham 35215-2010
205-853-1200

Gadsen State Community College
P.O. Box 227
Gadsden 35902-0227
205-549-8259

George C. Wallace State Community
College–Hanceville
801 Main St., P.O. Box 2000
Hanceville 35077-2000
205-352-8000

University of Alabama at Birmingham
619 South 19th St
Birmingham 35233
205-934-4011

Community College of the Air Force
Maxwell Air Force Base
Montgomery 36112
334-953-6436

ARIZONA
The Bryman School
4343 North 16th St.
Phoenix 85016
602-274-4300

Gateway Community College
108 North 40th St.
Phoenix 85034
602-392-5189

ARKANSAS
Sparks Regional Medical Center School
of Radiology
1311 South Eye St.
Fort Smith 72917-7006
501-441-5172

Carti School of Radiation Therapy
Technology
P.O. Box 5210
Little Rock 72215
501-660-7623

Arkansas Valley Technical Institute
Hwy. 23 N, P.O. Box 506
Ozark 72949
501-667-2117

CALIFORNIA
Cabrillo College
6500 Soquel Dr.
Apton 95003
408-479-6461

Orange Coast College
2701 Fairview Rd.
Costa Mesa 92626
714-432-5757

Cypress College
9200 Valley View
Cypress 90630
714-826-2220

Fresno City College
1101 East University Ave.
Fresno 93741
209-442-4600

American School of X-Ray
13723 Harvard Place
Gardena 90249
213-770-4001

Loma Linda University
Loma Linda 92350
909-824-4931

Educorp Career College
230 East Third St.
Long Beach 90802
310-437-0501

Long Beach City College
4901 East Carson St.
Long Beach 90808
310-420-4176

Foothill College
12345 El Monte Rd.
Los Altos Hills 94022
415-949-7469

Charles R. Drew University of Medicine and Science
1621 East 120th St.
Los Angeles 90059
213-563-5835

Nova Institute of Health Technology
2400 South Western Ave.
Los Angeles 90018
213-735-2222

Yuba College
2088 North Beale Rd.
Marysville 95901
916-741-6960

Merced College
3600 M St.
Merced 95348-2898
209-384-6132

Modern Technology School of X-Ray
6180 Laurel Canyon Blvd.
North Hollywood 91606
818-763-2563

Butte College
3536 Butte Campus Dr.
Oroville 95965
916-895-2511

Chaffey Community College
5885 Haven Ave.
Rancho Cucamonga 91737-3002
909-941-2359

San Diego Mesa College
7250 Mesa College Dr.
San Diego 92111-4998
619-627-2666

Cancer Foundation Schools of Technology
300 West Pueblo St.
Santa Barbara 93195
805-682-7300

Santa Barbara City College
721 Cliff Dr.
Santa Barbara 93109-4395
805-965-0581

Santa Rosa Junior College
1501 Mendocino Ave.
Santa Rosa 95401-4395
707-527-4346

San Joaquin General Hospital School of Radiation Technology
P.O. Box 1020
Stockton 95201
209-468-6233

Directory of Healthcare Programs

Mount San Antonio College
1100 North Grand
Walnut 91789
909-594-5611

Nova Institute of Health Technology
11416 Whittier Blvd.
Whittier 90601
310-695-0771

COLORADO
Community College of Denver
P.O. Box 173363
Denver 80217
303-556-2600

CONNECTICUT
Saint Vincent's Medical Center of Nuclear Medicine
2800 Main St.
Bridgeport 06606
203-576-5235

South Central Community College
60 Sargent Dr.
New Haven 06511
203-789-6928

DELAWARE
Delaware Technical and Community College Stanton-Wilmington
400 Stanton-Christiana Rd.
Newark 19713
302-454-3900

DISTRICT OF COLUMBIA
George Washington University
2121 I St. NW
Washington 20037
202-994-3725

FLORIDA
Santa Fe Community College
3000 Northwest 83rd St.
Gainesville 32601
904-395-5702

National School of Technology, Inc.
4355 West 16th Ave.
Hialeah 33012
305-945-2929

Jackson Memorial Medical Center
University of Miami
1611 NW 12th Ave.
Miami 33136
305-585-6811

Florida Hospital College of Health Sciences
800 Lake Estelle Dr.
Orlando 32803
407-895-7747

Palm Beach Community College
3160 PGA Blvd.
Palm Beach Gardens 324018-2893
407-625-2511

Pensacola Junior College
1000 College Blvd.
Pensacola 32504
904-476-5410

Hillsborough Community College
P.O. Box 31127
Tampa 33631-3127
813-253-7004

Saint Petersburg Junior College
P.O. Box 13489
Saint Petersburg 33733
813-546-0021

GEORGIA
Albany Technical Institute
1021 Lowe Rd.
Albany 31708
912-430-3500

Athens Area Technical Institute
899 Hwy 29 N
Athens 30601
706-542-8050

Emory University School of Medicine
1364 Clifton Rd., NE
Atlanta 30322
404-712-5512

Fulton De Kalb Hospital Authority Grady Memorial Hospital
80 Butler St., P.O. Box 26044
Atlanta 30335-3801
404-616-4307

Medical College of Georgia
1120 15th St.
Augusta 30912
706-721-0211

Brunswick College
3700 Altama Ave.
Brunswick 31520-3644
912-264-7235

Medical Center, Inc.–School of Radiologic Technology
710 Center St., P.O. Box Drawer 85
Columbus 31994-2299
404-571-1155

De Kalb Medical Center School of Radiation Technology
2701 North Decatur Rd.
Decatur 30033
404-297-5307

HAWAII

Kapiolani Community College
4303 Diamond Head Rd.
Honolulu 96816
808-956-6637

ILLINOIS

Belleville Area College
2500 Carlyle Rd.
Belleville 62221
618-235-2700

Southern Illinois University-Carbondale
Carbondale 62901
618-453-8882

Kaskaskia College
27210 College Rd.
Centralia 62801
618-532-1981

Cook County Hospital School of X-Ray Technology
1825 West Harrison St.
Chicago 60612
312-633-8522

College of Du Page
Lambert Rd. and 22nd St.
Glen Ellyn 60137
708-858-2800

Moraine Valley Community College
10900 South 88th Ave.
Paios Hills 60465-0937
708-974-5316

Methodist Medical Center of Illinois–Medical Technology
221 Northeast Glen Oak Ave.
Peoria 61636-0001
309-672-5513

Triton College
2000 Fifth Ave.
River Grove 60171
708-456-0300

Rockford Memorial Hospital School of X-Ray Technology
2400 North Rockton Ave.
Rockford 61103
815-969-5480

Swedish American Hospital School of Surgical Technology
1400 Charles St.
Rockford 61104-1257
815-968-4400

Directory of Healthcare Programs

INDIANA
Wellborn Cancer Center
401 Southeast Sixth St.
Evansville 47713
812-426-8321

Indiana University–Purdue University at Indianapolis
355 North Lansing
Indianapolis 46202
317-274-5555

Ball State University
2000 University Ave.
Muncie 48306
765-285-8300

IOWA
Scott Community College
500 Belmont Rd.
Bettendorf 52722-5649
319-359-7531

Jennie Edmundson Memorial Hospital
933 East Pierce St.
Council Bluffs 51503
712-328-6010

Iowa Methodist Medical Center
1200 Pleasant St.
Des Moines 50309
515-241-6171

Iowa Central Community College
(Fort Dodge Center)
330 Avenue "M"
Fort Dodge 50501
515-576-7201

University of Iowa
Iowa City 52242
319-335-3500

KANSAS
Fort Hays State University
600 Park St.
Hays 67601-4099
913-628-4222

Labette Community College
200 South 14th
Parsons 67357
316-421-6700

Washburn University of Topeka
1700 College Ave.
Topeka 66621
913-231-1010

KENTUCKY
Kentucky Technical–Bowling Green
State Vocational Technical School
1845 Loop Dr., P.O. Box 6000
Bowling Green 42101
502-781-0711

Lexington Community College
Cooper Dr.
Lexington 40506
606-257-4831

Morehead State University
University Blvd.
Morehead 40351
606-783-2655

LOUISIANA
Delgado Community College
615 City Park Ave.
New Orleans 70119
504-483-4114

MAINE
Southern Maine Technical College
Fort Rd.
South Portland 04106
207-767-9520

MARYLAND
Essex Community College
7201 Rossville Rd.
Baltimore 21237
410-780-6363

Prince Georges Community College
301 Largo Rd.
Largo 23701-1243
301-322-0819

MASSACHUSETTS
Bunker Hill Community College
New Rutherford Ave.
Boston 02129
617-228-2027

Northeastern University
360 Huntington Ave.
Boston 02115
617-373-2525

Massasoit Community College
One Massasoit Blvd.
Brockton 02402
508-588-9100

Holyoke Community College
303 Homestead Ave.
Holyoke 01040
413-538-7000

Springfield Technical Community College
Armory Square
Springfield 01105
413-781-7822

MICHIGAN
Ferris State University
901 South State Rd.
Big Rapids 49307
616-592-2000

Grand Rapids Community College
143 Bostwick Ave. NE
Grand Rapids 49505
616-456-4965

Lansing Community College
419 North Capitol Ave.
Lansing 48901-7210
517-483-1200

William Beaumont Hospital
3601 West 13 Mile Rd.
Royal Oak 48073-6769
810-551-5000

Carnegie Institute
550 Stephenson Hwy.
Troy 48083
810-589-1078

MINNESOTA
Northwest Technical College-East Grand Forks
Hwy. 220 N
East Grand Forks 56721
218-773-3441

Mayo School of Health-Related Sciences
200 First St. SW
Rochester 55905
507-284-3678

Rochester Community College
851 30th Ave. SE
Rochester 55904-4999
507-285-7210

MISSISSIPPI
University of Mississippi Medical Center
2500 North State St.
Jackson 39216
601-876-3500

Directory of Healthcare Programs

MISSOURI
Research Medical Center School of Nuclear Medical Technology
2316 East Meyer Blvd.
Kansas City 64132
816-276-3390

Saint Luke's College
4426 Wornall Rd.
Kansas City 64111
816-932-2233

Saint Louis Community College–Forest Park
5600 Oakland Ave.
Saint Louis 63110
314-644-9280

NEW HAMPSHIRE
New Hampshire Technical Institute
11 Institute Dr.
Concord 03301
603-225-1865

NEW JERSEY
Hudson Area School of Radiologic Technology
29 East 29th St.
Bayonne 07002
201-858-5348

Middlesex County College
155 Mill Rd., P.O. Box 3050
Edison 08818-3050
908-548-6000

University of Medicine and Dentistry of New Jersey
65 Bergen St.
Newark 07107
201-982-4821

Bergen Community College
400 Paramus Rd.
Paramus 07652
201-447-7178

Overlook Hospital School of Nuclear Medical Technology
99 Beauvoir Ave., P.O. Box 220
Summit 07902-0220
908-522-2072

NEW YORK
Broome Community College
P.O. Box 1017
Binghamton 13902
607-778-5000

CUNY New York City Technical College
300 Jay St.
Brooklyn 11201
718-260-5560

Trocaire College
110 Red Jackey Pkwy.
Buffalo 14220
716-826-1200

Nassau Community College
One Education Dr.
Garden City 11530
516-572-7345

Bellevue Hospital Center School of Radiation Technology
First Ave. and 27th St.
New York 10016

PENNSYLVANIA
North Hills School of Health Occupations
1500 Northway Mall
Pittsburgh 15237
412-367-8003

Crozer-Chester Medical Center–Allied Health Program
One Medical Center Blvd.
Upland 19013
610-447-2000

Wilkes-Barre General Hospital–School
of Medical Technology
North River and Aufurn
Wilkes-Barre 18764
717-820-2737

RHODE ISLAND
Rhode Island Hospital School of
Nuclear Medicine
593 Eddy St.
Providence 02903
401-444-5724

Community College of Rhode Island
400 East Ave.
Warwick 02886-1805
401-825-1000

SOUTH CAROLINA
Trident Technical College
P.O. Box 118067
Charleston 29423-8067
803-572-6111

Horry-Georgetown Technical College
P.O. Box 1966
Conway 29526
803-347-3186

Greenville Technical College
Station B, P.O. Box 5616
Greenville 29606-5616
803-250-8000

TENNESSEE
Chattanooga State Technical
Community College
4501 Amnicola Hwy.
Chattanooga 37406
615-697-4401

Roane State Community College
276 Patton Ln.
Harriman 37748
615-882-4501

East Tennessee State University
P.O. Box 70716
Johnson City 37614
423-929-4112

Shelby State Community College
P.O. Box 40568
Memphis 38174-0568
901-544-5000

TEXAS
Amarillo College
P.O. Box 447
Amarillo 79178
806-354-6071

Austin Community College
5930 Middle Fiskville Rd.
Austin 78782
512-223-7504

Lamar University–Beaumont
4400 MLK, P.O. Box 10001
Beaumont 77710
409-880-8845

El Centro College
Main and Lamar
Dallas 75202
214-746-2278

El Paso Community College
P.O. Box 20500
El Paso 79998
915-594-2000

Moncrief Radiation Center School of
Radiation Therapy
1450 Eighth Ave.
Fort Worth 76104
817-923-7393

Galveston College
4015 Ave. Q
Galveston 77550
409-772-9467

Houston Community College System
22 Waugh Dr., P.O. Box 7849
Houston 77270-7849
713-869-5021

Ultrasound Diagnostic School
580 Decker Drive
Irving 75062
214-791-1120

San Jacinto College–Central Campus
8060 Spencer Hwy.
Pasadena 77505
713-476-1871

Saint Philip's College
1801 Martin Luther King Dr.
San Antonio 78203
512-531-3591

McLennan Community College
1400 College Dr.
Waco 76708
817-750-3542

Midwestern State University
3410 Taft Blvd.
Wichita Falls 76308-2099
817-689-4608

UTAH
Utah Valley Hospital School of
Radiologic Technology
1034 North Fifth West St.
Provo 84603
801-373-7850

VIRGINIA
Tidewater Community College
Rte. 135
Portsmouth 23703
804-484-2121

WASHINGTON
Bellevue Community College
3000 Landerholm Circle SE
Bellevue 98007-6484
206-641-0111

Tacoma Community College
5900 South 12th St.
Tacoma 98465
206-756-5000

Yakima Valley Community College
P.O. Box 1647
Yakima 98907
509-575-2373

WEST VIRGINIA
West Virginia University Hospital School
of Radiation Technology
Medical Center Dr., P.O. Box 8062
Morgantown 26506-8062
304-598-4252

WISCONSIN
Milwaukee Area Technical College
700 West State St.
Milwaukee 53233
414-297-6600

Saint Joseph's Hospital School of
Medical Technology
611 Saint Joseph's Ave.
Marshfield 54449
715-387-7202

Saint Luke's Medical Center School of
Diagnostic Medical Sonography
2900 West Oklahoma Ave.
Milwaukee 53215
414-649-6762

Mercy Medical Center School of
Radiologic Technology
631 Hazel St.
Oshkosh 54902
414-236-2253

SURGICAL TECHNOLOGY

ALABAMA
Community College of the Air Force
Maxwell Air Force Base
Montgomery 36112
334-953-6436

ARIZONA
The Bryman School
4343 North 16th St.
Phoenix 85016
602-274-4300

CALIFORNIA
California Paramedic and Technical College
3745 Long Beach Blvd.
Long Beach 90807
310-595-6630

ConCorde Career Intitute
4150 Lankershim Blvd.
North Hollywood, CA 91602
818-766-8151

Hospital Consortium of San Mateo County
Surgical Technologist Program
1600 Trousdale Drive
Burlington, CA 94010
415-696-7872

Institute of Business and Medical Technology
75-110 Saint Charles Place
Palm Desert 92260
818-597-8490

Loma Linda University
Nichol Hall, Room 1926
Loma Linda, CA 92350
909-824-4932

Naval School of Health Sciences - San Diego
Surgical Technologist Program
San Diego, CA 92134-5291
619-532-7821

Newbridge College
700 El Camino Real
Tustin 92680
714-573-8787

Simi Valley Adult School
3192 Los Angeles Avenue
Simi Valley, CA 93065
805-527-4840

Southwestern Community College
900 Otay Lakes Road
Chula Vista, CA 91910
619-421-6700

COLORADO
Concorde Career Institute
770 Grant St.
Denver 80203
303-861-1151

FLORIDA
Daytona Beach Community College
Surgical Technologist Program
P.O. Box 2811
1200 International Speedway Blvd.
Daytona Beach, FL 32120
904-255-8131

Traviss Technical Center
3225 Winter Lake Road
Lakeland, FL 33803
941-499-2700

Lindsey Hopkins Tech Education Center
Surgical Technologist Program
750 NW 20th Street
Miami, FL 33127
305-324-6070

Directory of Healthcare Programs

Central Florida Community College
Surgical Technologist Program
P.O. Box 1388
Ocala, FL 34478-1388
904-237-2111

Orlando Technical Center
301 West Amelia
Orlando, FL 32801
407-425-2756

Sheridan Vocational Center
5400 West Sheridan St.
Hollywood 33021
954-985-3220

David G. Erwin Technical Center
Surgical Technologist Program
2010 East Hillsborough Avenue
Tampa, FL 33610-8299
813-231-1800

GEORGIA
Athens Area Technical Institute
800 Hwy. 29 N
Athens 30601
706-542-8050

ILLINOIS
Swedish American Hospital School of Surgical Technology
1400 Charles St.
Rockford 61104-1257
815-968-4400

KENTUCKY
Kentucky Department for Adult & Technical Education-Central Kentucky SVTS
104 Vo-Tech Rd.
Lexington 40510
606-255-8501

Kentucky Technical–Jefferson State Vocational Technical School
727 West Chestnut
Louisville 40203
502-595-4221

LOUISIANA
Delgado Community College
615 City Park Ave.
New Orleans 70119
504-483-4114

MASSACHUSETTS
Quincy College
Surgical Technologist Program
School of Allied Health
50 Saville Road
Quincy, MA 02169
617-984-1647

New England Baptist Hospital School of Nursing
220 Fisher Ave.
Boston 02120
617-739-5260

Quincy College
34 Coddington St.
Quincy 02169
617-984-1600

Springfield Tech Community College
Surgical Technologist Program
One Armory Square
Springfield, MA 01105
413-781-7822

Worcester Technical Institute
Surgical Technologist Program
251 Belmont Street
Worcester, MA 01605
508-799-1945

MICHIGAN
Lansing Community College
419 North Capitol Ave.
Lansing 48901-7201
517-483-9850

MINNESOTA
Northwest Technical College–East Grand Forks
Hwy. 220 N
East Grand Forks 56721
218-773-3441

Minnesota Riverland Technical College–Rochester Campus
1926 College View Rd. SE
Rochester 55904
507-285-8631

Saint Cloud Technical College
1540 Northway Dr.
Saint Cloud 56303
612-654-5000

MISSISSIPPI
Itawamba Community College
602 West Hill St.
Fulton 38843
601-862-3101

NEW YORK
Nassau Community College
1 Education Drive
Garden City, NY 11530
516-572-7914

New York University Medical Center
Center for Allied Health Education
550 First Avenue
New York, NY 10016
212-263-5007

Niagara County Community College
P.O. Box 5236
3111 Saunders Settlement Road
Sanborn, NY 14132
716-731-4101

Onondaga Community College
Onandoga Road
Syracuse, NY 13215
315-469-7741

Trocaire College
110 Red Jacket Parkway
Buffalo, NY 14220
716-862-1200

PENNSYLVANIA
Mount Aloysius College
One College Dr.
Cresson 16630-1999
814-886-4131

Delaware County Community College
901 South Media Line Rd.
Media 19063
610-359-5000

Saint Francis Medical Center School of Nursing
400 45th St.
Pittsburgh 15201
412-622-4494

Wilkes-Barre General Hospital-School of Medical Technology
North River and Auburn
Wilkes-Barre 18764
717-820-2737

SOUTH CAROLINA
Midlands Technical College
P.O. Box 2408
Columbia 29202
803-738-8324

York Technical College
452 South Anderson Rd.
Rock Hill 29730
803-327-8000

Directory of Healthcare Programs

TENNESSEE
Knoxville State Area Vocational-Technical School
1100 Liberty St.
Knoxville 37919
615-546-5568

Memphis Area Vocational-Technical School
550 Alabama Ave.
Memphis 38105-3799
901-543-6100

Aquinas Junior College
4210 Harding Rd.
Nashville 37205
615-297-7545

TEXAS
Texas State Technical College–Harlingen Campus
2424 Boxwood
Harlingen 78550-3697
210-425-0600

Houston Community College System
22 Waugh Dr., P.O. Box 7849
Houston 77270-7849
713-869-5021

South Plains College
1401 College Ave.
Levelland 79336
806-894-9611

San Antonio College of Medical and Dental Assistants
5280 Medical Dr.
San Antonio 78229
210-692-0241

Temple Junior College
2600 South First St.
Temple 76504-7435
817-773-9961

VIRGINIA
NNPS RRMC School of Surgical Technology
12420 Warwick Blvd.
Newport News 23606
757-594-2722

WASHINGTON
Seattle Central Community College
1701 Broadway
Seattle 98122
206-587-3800

WISCONSIN
Northeast Wisconsin Technical Center
2740 West Mason St., P.O. Box 19042
Green Bay 54307-9042
414-498-5400

CHAPTER | 4

FINANCIAL AID FOR THE TRAINING YOU NEED

> This chapter explains how to receive financial aid from the school you wish to attend. You'll find information on how to gather your financial records, determine your eligibility for financial aid, distinguish between different types of financial aid, and file your forms once you have completed them. Sample financial aid forms and interviews from financial aid advisors and students who have received aid will help guide you through the process.

Many potential students think they can't afford college because of the high costs. It may cost $15,000 or more a year to go to a major university; smaller colleges cost close to $2,000 a year plus books and living expenses. Before you attend a training school or college, you have to figure out if you can afford classes, books, and any extracurricular classes you want to take. You should explore the financial aid opportunities that are available to help you pay for the training program you want.

GETTING STARTED

Every school has a financial aid department. This is where you can obtain a financial aid application called the Free Application for Federal Student Aid (FAFSA). You can also contact the U.S. Department of Education at 800-433-3242 to receive an application by mail. You should get this application right away; it determines your eligibility status for all grants and loans provided by federal or state governments and certain college or institution aid.

Amazingly enough, you can attend a small college or even a university without paying a dime if you know what to do and if you can establish adequate financial need. One nursing student from Dallas, Texas, explains how she did it:

> I researched carefully what kind of aid I might be eligible to receive. I have a small child, so I knew my expenses would be tight. I applied for and received the Pell Grant and the Hope Scholarship. Between the two types of aid, I have money left over for books and some daycare expenses. I work part time for money to live on day to day and to pay bills, but I am getting an education basically tuition-free.

Determining Your Eligibility

To receive financial aid from an accredited college or institution's student aid program, you must:

- have financial need, except for some loan programs
- have a high school diploma or a General Education Development (GED) Certificate, pass a test approved by the U.S Department of Education, or meet other standards your state establishes that are approved by the U.S. Department of Education
- be enrolled or accepted for enrollment as a regular student working toward a degree or certificate in an eligible program
- be a U.S. citizen or eligible non-citizen
- have a valid social security number
- make satisfactory academic progress
- sign a statement of educational purpose and a certification statement on overpayment and default
- register with selective services, if required

When to Apply

Apply for financial aid as soon as possible after January 1 of the year in which you want to enroll in school. For example, if you want to begin school in the fall of 1998, then you should apply for financial aid as soon as possible after January 1, 1998. It is easier to complete the application when you already have your

Financial Aid for the Training You Need

completed tax return, so consider filing your taxes as early as possible as well. Do not sign, date, or send your application before January 1 of the year for which you are seeking aid. If you apply by mail, send your completed application in the envelope that came with it. The envelope is already addressed, and using it will ensure that your application reaches the correct address.

You must reapply for financial aid every year. However, after your first year, you will receive a Student Aid Report in the mail before the application deadline. If it needs no corrections, you can just sign it and send it in.

Many students lose out on thousands of dollars in grants and loans because they file too late. A financial aid counselor from William Paterson College in New Jersey suggests:

> When you fill out the Free Application for Federal Student Aid (FAFSA), you are applying for all aid available, both federal and state, work-study, student loans, etc. The important thing is complying with the deadline date. Those students who do are considered for the Pell Grant, the SEOG (Supplemental Educational Opportunity Grant), and the Perkins Loan, which is the best loan as far as interest goes. Lots of students miss the June 30 deadline, and it can mean losing $2,480 from TAG, about $350 from WPCNJ, and another $1,100 from EOF. Students, usually the ones who need the money most, often ignore the deadlines.

Getting Your Forms Filed

Filing your forms is as simple as remembering the following:

1. Pay attention to the deadlines. There are no exceptions to the June 30 deadline to apply for the next year.
2. Fill out the forms as completely as possible. Make an appointment with a financial aid counselor if you need help.

Many financial aid counselors gripe that students don't read the forms completely and don't file early. Your success in your career depends on how serious you are about working toward your goal. This is just one more part of your goal, so don't let lack of money be the excuse for not attending school.

If you apply electronically through a school, your application will be processed in about a week. If you apply by mail, your application will be processed in approximately four weeks. Then you will receive a Student Aid Report (SAR) in the mail. The SAR will report the information from your application, and if there are no questions or problems with your application, your SAR will report your Expected Family Contribution (EFC), the number used in determining your eligibility for federal student aid. Each school you list on the application also will get your application information if the school can receive the information electronically.

Financial Need

Aid from most of the programs discussed in this chapter is awarded on the basis of financial need (except unsubsidized Stafford and all PLUS and Consolidation loans). When you apply for federal student aid, the information you report is used in a formula established by the U.S. Congress. The formula determines your Expected Family Contribution (EFC), an amount you and your family are expected to contribute toward your education. If your EFC is below a certain amount, you'll be eligible for a Federal Pell Grant, assuming you meet all other eligibility requirements.

There isn't a maximum EFC that defines eligibility for the other financial aid options. Instead, your EFC is used in an equation to determine your financial needs.

> **Cost of Attendance − EFC = Financial Need**

Your financial aid administrator calculates your cost of attendance and subtracts the amount you and your family are expected to contribute toward that cost. If there's anything left over, you're considered to have financial need.

Gathering Financial Records

Your financial need for grants or loans depends on your financial standing. When you apply for aid, your answers to certain questions will determine whether you're considered dependent on your parents, in which case you must report their income and assets as well as your own, or independent, in which case you must report only your own income and assets (and those of your spouse if you're married).

Financial Aid for the Training You Need

You're an independent student if at least one of the following applies to you:

- You were born before January 1, 1974
- You're married
- You have legal dependents other than a spouse
- You're an orphan or ward of the court (or were a ward of the court until age 18)
- You're a veteran of the U.S. Armed Forces

If you live with your parents and if they claimed you as a dependent on their last tax return, then your need will be based on your parents' income. Students are classified as dependent or independent because federal student aid programs are based on the idea that students (and their parents or spouse, if applicable) have the primary responsibility for paying for their postsecondary education.

You will need to gather your tax records for the year prior to the year for which you are applying. For example, if you apply for the fall of 1999, you will use your tax records from 1998.

TYPES OF FINANCIAL AID

Many types of financial aid are available to help with school expenses. Most financial aid is determined by need. You do not have to pay back grants or scholarships. Grants and any outside scholarships will be factored in to your application profile to determine if you require any interest-bearing loans. For more detailed information about each type of assistance, see your financial aid counselor and the financial aid booklet you receive with your application.

Scholarships

Different types of scholarships are available for any type of program you may enter, and many institutions offer scholarships most students do not know about. Each state has different available scholarships, and private scholarships are awarded on a regular basis. For more information on scholarships, contact your financial aid counselor. See Appendix A for addresses of scholarships listed here. To find books that offer extensive listings of scholarships, see Appendix B or your local library or bookstore. Examples of state scholarships include but are not limited to the following:

- The Hope Scholarship is a Georgia lottery funded scholarship for students who keep at least a 3.0 grade point average.
- The New Hampshire Charitable Fund Student Aid Program offers scholarships to New Hampshire residents.
- The Illinois Hospital Association Scholarship is offered to Illinois residents with a 3.5 GPA or higher.

Military scholarships are also available if you are applying to the Army, Navy, Air Force, or Marines; these include the G.I. Bill and other money for college or to pay off previous loans.

There are also private scholarships, such as the following:
- Maxine Williams Scholarships from the American Association of Medical Assistants Endowment.
- The American Medical Technologist Scholarship awards $250 to high school students or graduates in good standing.
- The American Association of Homes for the Aging offers Nurse Education Scholarships.
- The Dental Assisting Scholarship Program, part of the ADA Endowment Fund and Assistance, offers scholarships.

See Appendix A for more association addresses and phone numbers.

A financial aid counselor from William Paterson College in New Jersey says:

> I get notices of many scholarships for health careers. I publish them in the school paper and on the TV and radio stations on campus. I also refer students to the nursing department, which posts scholarships sent directly there. Schools also offer minority scholarships, trustee scholarships, and presidential scholarships. The state of New Jersey offers the Garden State Scholarship for Garden State distinguished scholars. The college will match you to the available scholarships. Deadline dates are important. The most important thing you can do for yourself is apply early.

Federal Pell Grants

A Federal Pell Grant, unlike a loan, does not have to be repaid. Pell Grants are awarded only to undergraduate students who have not yet earned a bachelor's or professional degree. For many students, Pell Grants provide a foundation of financial aid to which other aid may be added.

Awards for the award year will depend on program funding. The maximum award for the 1996–1997 award year was $2,470. You can receive only one Pell Grant in an award year. How much you get will depend not only on your EFC but also on your cost of attendance, whether you're a full-time or part-time student, and whether you attend school for a full academic year or less. You cannot receive Pell Grant funds for more than one school at a time.

Federal Supplemental Educational Opportunity Grants (FSEOG)

A Federal Supplemental Educational Opportunity Grant (FSEOG) is for undergraduates with exceptional financial need—that is, students with the lowest Expected Family Contributions (EFCs)—and gives priority to students who receive Federal Pell Grants. An FSEOG doesn't have to be paid back.

You can receive between $100 and $4,000 a year, depending on when you apply, your level of need, and the funding level of the school you're attending. There's no guarantee every eligible student will be able to receive a FSEOG. Students at each school are paid based on the availability of funds at that school; not all schools participate in the program.

Federal Work-Study Program

The Federal Work-Study Program provides jobs for undergraduate and graduate students with financial need and allows them to earn money to help pay education expenses. The program encourages community service work and provides hands-on experience related to your course of study.

Your work-study salary will be at least the current federal minimum wage or higher, depending on the type of work you do and the skills required. Your total award depends on when you apply, your level of need, and the funding level of your school. Not all schools have work-study in every area of study.

Federal Perkins Loans

A Federal Perkins Loan has the lowest interest (5 percent) of any loan available for both undergraduate and graduate students with exceptional financial need. Your school is your lender, and the loan is made with government funds. You must repay this loan to your school.

Depending on when you apply, your level of need, and the funding level of the school, you can borrow up to $3,000 for each year of undergraduate study. The total amount you can borrow as an undergraduate is $15,000.

PLUS Loans (Loans for Parents)

PLUS loans enable parents with good credit histories to borrow money to pay education expenses of a child who is a dependent undergraduate student enrolled at least half time. PLUS loans are available through both the Direct Loan and FFEL programs (explained in the next section). Your parents must submit the completed forms to your school.

To be eligible, your parents will be required to pass a credit check. If they don't pass the credit check, they may still be able to receive a loan if they can prove extenuating circumstances or if someone who is able to pass the credit check agrees to co-sign the loan. Your parents must also meet citizenship requirements.

The yearly limit on a PLUS Loan is equal to your cost of attendance minus any other financial aid you receive. For instance, if your cost of attendance is $6,000 and you receive $4,000 in other financial aid, your parents can borrow up to, but no more than, $2,000.

Direct and Federal Family Education Loan (FFEL) Stafford Loans

Direct and FFEL Stafford Loans are a major form of financial aid. Direct Stafford Loans are available through the William D. Ford Federal Direct Loan Program, and FFEL Stafford Loans are available through the Federal Family Education Loan Program. The major differences between the two are the source of the loan funds, some aspects of the application process, and the available repayment plans.

Direct and FFEL Stafford Loans are either subsidized or unsubsidized. A *subsidized* loan is awarded on the basis of financial need. You will not be charged any interest before you begin repayment or during authorized periods of deferment. The federal government "subsidizes" the interest during these periods.

An *unsubsidized* loan is not awarded on the basis of need. You'll be charged interest from the time the loan is disbursed until it is paid in full. If you allow the interest to accumulate, it will be capitalized—that is, the interest will be added to the principal amount of your loan, and additional interest will be based on the higher amount. This will increase the amount you have to repay.

If you're a dependent undergraduate student, you can borrow up to:

- $2,625 if you're a first-year student enrolled in a program that is at least a full academic year
- $3,500 if you've completed your first year of study and the remainder of your program is at least a full academic year
- $5,500 a year if you've completed two years of study and the remainder of your program is at least a full academic year

If you're an independent undergraduate student or a dependent student whose parents are unable to get a PLUS Loan, you can borrow up to:

- $6,625 if you're a first-year student enrolled in a program that is at least a full academic year
- $7,500 if you've completed your first year of study and the remainder of your program is at least a full academic year

Loan Repayment

If you receive any interest-bearing student loans, after graduation you will attend exit counseling, during which the loan lenders will tell you your total debt and work out a payment schedule with you. Many loans include a grace period, so you don't have to start paying them off for at least six to nine months after you graduate. For example, you do not have to begin repaying the Perkins Loan until nine months after you graduate. This grace period gives you time to find a good job and start earning money. During this time, you may have to pay the interest on your loan.

Repayment schedules differ according to your salary. You can begin repaying the highest amount available or opt for a graduated repayment schedule. A graduated repayment schedule allows you to start with small payments that will increase as your salary level increases. If for some reason you remain unemployed when your payments become due, you may receive an unemployment deferment for a certain length of time. For many of these loans, you will have a maximum repayment period of 10 years (excluding periods of deferment and forbearance).

Consolidating Loans for Repayment

A consolidation loan is designed to help student and parent borrowers simplify loan repayment by allowing the borrower to consolidate several types of federal student loans with various repayment schedules into one loan. The interest rate on the consolidation loan may be lower than what you're currently paying on one or more of your loans. The phone number for loan consolidation at the William D. Ford Direct Loan Program is 800-557-7392. Financial administrators recommend that you do not consolidate a Perkins Loan with any other loans since the interest on a Perkins Loan is already the lowest available.

Helpful Telephone Numbers and Web Sites

If you need immediate answers to questions about federal student aid or application forms, call the hotline number 800-433-3243 at the Federal Student Aid Information Center between 9 a.m. and 8 p.m. (Eastern time), Monday through Friday. If you're hearing impaired, call 800-730-8913, a toll-free TDD number at the Information Center.

The Student Guide is also available online at the Department of Education's web address: www.ed.gov/prog_info/SFAStudentGuide.

Help in completing the FAFSA is available online too at www.ed.gov/prog_info/SFA/FAFSA.

A list of Title IV school codes that you may need to complete the FAFSA is available at www.ed.gov/offices/OPE/t4_codes.html.

The following phone numbers may be of help as you fill out your forms:

Selective Service   847-688-6888

Immigration and Naturalization   415-705-4205

Internal Revenue Service   800-829-1040

Social Security Administration   800-772-1213

National Merit Scholarship Corporation   708-866-5100

Sallie Mae's College AnswerSM Service   800-222-7183

Financial Aid for the Training You Need

Free Application for Federal Student Aid
1997–98 School Year

WARNING: If you purposely give false or misleading information on this form, you may be fined $10,000, sent to prison, or both.

"You" and "your" on this form always mean the student who wants aid.

Form Approved
OMB No. 1840-0110
App. Exp. 6/30/98

U.S. Department of Education
Student Financial Assistance Programs

Use dark ink. Make capital letters and numbers clear and legible.   E X M 2 4   Fill in ovals completely. Only one oval per question.   Correct ●   Incorrect marks will be ignored.   Incorrect ⊗ ✓

Section A: You (the student)

1–3. Your name
1. Last name
2. First name
3. M.I.

Your title (optional)   Mr. ○1   Miss, Mrs., or Ms. ○2

4–7. Your permanent mailing address
(All mail will be sent to this address. See Instructions, page 2 for state/country abbreviations.)
4. Number and street (Include apt. no.)
5. City
6. State
7. ZIP code

8. Your social security number (SSN) *(Don't leave blank. See Instructions, page 2.)*

9. Your date of birth   Month Day Year 1 9

10. Your permanent home telephone number   Area code

11. Your state of legal residence   State

12. Date you became a legal resident of the state in question 11 *(See Instructions, page 2.)*   Month Day Year 1 9

13–14. Your driver's license number *(Include the state abbreviation. If you don't have a license, write in "None.")*
State   License number

15–16. Are you a U.S. citizen? *(See Instructions, pages 2–3.)*
Yes, I am a U.S. citizen. ○1
No, but I am an eligible noncitizen. ○2
A
No, neither of the above. ○3

17. As of today, are you married? *(Fill in only one oval.)*
I am not married. (I am single, widowed, or divorced.) ○1
I am married. ○2
I am separated from my spouse. ○3

18. Date you were married, separated, divorced, or widowed. If divorced, use date of divorce or separation, whichever is earlier. *(If never married, leave blank.)*   Month Year 1 9

19. Will you have your first bachelor's degree before July 1, 1997?   Yes ○1   No ○2

Section B: Education Background

20–21. Date that you (the student) received, or will receive, your high school diploma, either—
(Enter one date. Leave blank if the question does not apply to you.)
- by graduating from high school   **20.** Month Year 1 9
OR
- by earning a GED   **21.** Month Year 1 9

22–23. Highest educational level or grade level your father and your mother completed. *(Fill in one oval for each parent. See Instructions, page 3.)*

	22. Father	23. Mother
elementary school (K–8)	○1	○1
high school (9–12)	○2	○2
college or beyond	○3	○3
unknown	○4	○4

If you (and your family) have **unusual circumstances**, complete this form and then check with your financial aid administrator. Examples:
- tuition expenses at an elementary or secondary school,
- unusual medical or dental expenses not covered by insurance,
- a family member who recently became unemployed, or
- other unusual circumstances such as changes in income or assets that might affect your eligibility for student financial aid.

109

Healthcare Career Starter

Section C: Your Plans *Answer these questions about your college plans.* Page 2

24–28. Your expected enrollment status for the 1997–98 school year
(See Instructions, page 3.)

School term	Full time	3/4 time	1/2 time	Less than 1/2 time	Not enrolled
24. Summer term '97	○ 1	○ 2	○ 3	○ 4	○ 5
25. Fall semester/qtr. '97	○ 1	○ 2	○ 3	○ 4	○ 5
26. Winter quarter '97-98	○ 1	○ 2	○ 3	○ 4	○ 5
27. Spring semester/qtr. '98	○ 1	○ 2	○ 3	○ 4	○ 5
28. Summer term '98	○ 1	○ 2	○ 3	○ 4	○ 5

29. Your course of study *(See Instructions for code, page 3.)* Code ☐

30. College degree/certificate you expect to receive *(See Instructions for code, page 3.)* ☐

31. Date you expect to receive your degree/certificate   Month Day Year

32. Your grade level during the 1997–98 school year *(Fill in only one.)*
- 1st yr./never attended college ○ 1
- 1st yr./attended college before ○ 2
- 2nd year/sophomore ○ 3
- 3rd year/junior ○ 4
- 4th year/senior ○ 5
- 5th year/other undergraduate ○ 6
- 1st year graduate/professional ○ 7
- 2nd year graduate/professional ○ 8
- 3rd year graduate/professional ○ 9
- Beyond 3rd year graduate/professional ○ 10

33–35. In addition to grants, what other types of financial aid are you (and your parents) interested in? *(See Instructions, page 3.)*

	Yes	No
33. Student employment	○ 1	○ 2
34. Student loans	○ 1	○ 2
35. Parent loans for students	○ 1	○ 2

36. If you are (or were) in college, do you plan to attend **that same college** in 1997–98? *(If this doesn't apply to you, leave blank.)*   Yes ○ 1   No ○ 2

37. For how many dependents will you (the student) pay child care or elder care expenses in 1997–98? ☐

38–39. Veterans education benefits you expect to receive from July 1, 1997 through June 30, 1998

38. Amount per month $ ☐ .00

39. Number of months ☐

Section D: Student Status

		Yes	No
40.	Were you born **before** January 1, 1974?	○ 1	○ 2
41.	Are you a veteran of the U.S. Armed Forces?	○ 1	○ 2
42.	Will you be enrolled in a graduate or professional program (beyond a bachelor's degree) in 1997–98?	○ 1	○ 2
43.	Are you married?	○ 1	○ 2
44.	Are you an orphan or a ward of the court, or **were** you a ward of the court until age 18?	○ 1	○ 2
45.	Do you have legal dependents (**other than a spouse**) that fit the definition in Instructions, page 4?	○ 1	○ 2

If you answered **"Yes"** to **any** question in Section D, go to Section E and fill out **both the GRAY and the WHITE** areas on the rest of this form.

If you answered **"No"** to **every** question in Section D, go to Section E and fill out **both the GREEN and the WHITE** areas on the rest of this form.

Section E: Household Information

Remember:
At least one "Yes" answer in Section D means fill out the **GRAY** and WHITE areas.

All "No" answers in Section D means fill out the **GREEN** and WHITE areas.

STUDENT (& SPOUSE)

46. Number in your household in 1997–98 *(Include yourself and your spouse. Do not include your children and other people unless they meet the definition in Instructions, page 4.)* ☐

47. Number of college students in household in 1997–98 *(Of the number in 46, how many will be in college at least half-time in at least one term in an eligible program? Include yourself. See Instructions, page 4.)* ☐

PARENT(S)

48. Your parent(s)' **current** marital status:
- single ○ 1
- married ○ 2
- separated ○ 3
- divorced ○ 4
- widowed ○ 5

49. Your parent(s)' state of legal residence   State ☐

50. Date your parent(s) became legal resident(s) of the state in question 49 *(See Instructions, page 5.)*   Month Day Year 1 9

51. Number in your parent(s) household in 1997–98 *(Include yourself and your parents. Do not include your parents' other children and other people unless they meet the definition in Instructions, page 5.)* ☐

52. Number of college students in household in 1997–98 *(Of the number in 51, how many will be in college at least half-time in at least one term in an eligible program? Include yourself. See Instructions, page 5.)* ☐

Financial Aid for the Training You Need

Section F: 1996 Income, Earnings, and Benefits *You must see Instructions, pages 5 and 6, for information about tax forms and tax filing status, especially if you are estimating taxes or filing electronically or by telephone. These instructions will tell you what income and benefits should be reported in this section.*

Page 3

	STUDENT (& SPOUSE)	PARENT(S)
The following 1996 U.S. income tax figures are from:	*Everyone must fill out this column.* **53.** *(Fill in one oval.)*	**65.** *(Fill in one oval.)*
A—a completed 1996 IRS Form 1040A, 1040EZ, or 1040TEL	A ○ 1	A ○ 1
B—a completed 1996 IRS Form 1040	B ○ 2	B ○ 2
C—an estimated 1996 IRS Form 1040A, 1040EZ, or 1040TEL	C ○ 3	C ○ 3
D—an estimated 1996 IRS Form 1040	D ○ 4	D ○ 4
E—will not file a 1996 U.S. income tax return	*(Skip to question 57.)* ○ 5	*(Skip to 69.)* ○ 5

1996 Total number of exemptions (Form 1040–line 6d, or 1040A–line 6d; 1040EZ filers— *see Instructions, page 6.*) **54.** [ ]   **66.** [ ]

1996 Adjusted Gross Income (AGI; Form 1040–line 31, 1040A–line 16, or 1040EZ–line 4—*see Instructions, page 6.*) **55.** $ [ ].00   **67.** $ [ ].00

1996 U.S. income tax **paid** (Form 1040–line 44, 1040A–line 25, or 1040EZ–line 10) **56.** $ [ ].00   **68.** $ [ ].00

TAX FILERS ONLY

1996 Income earned from work (Student) **57.** $ [ ].00   (Father) **69.** $ [ ].00

1996 Income earned from work (Spouse) **58.** $ [ ].00   (Mother) **70.** $ [ ].00

1996 Untaxed income and benefits (yearly totals only):

Earned Income Credit (Form 1040–line 54, Form 1040A–line 29c, or Form 1040EZ–line 8) **59.** $ [ ].00   **71.** $ [ ].00

Untaxed Social Security Benefits **60.** $ [ ].00   **72.** $ [ ].00

Aid to Families with Dependent Children (AFDC/ADC) **61.** $ [ ].00   **73.** $ [ ].00

Child support received for all children **62.** $ [ ].00   **74.** $ [ ].00

Other untaxed income and benefits from Worksheet #2, page 11 **63.** $ [ ].00   **75.** $ [ ].00

1996 Amount from Line 5, Worksheet #3, page 12 *(See Instructions.)* **64.** $ [ ].00   **76.** $ [ ].00

Section G: Asset Information   **ATTENTION!**

Fill out Worksheet A or Worksheet B in Instructions, page 7. *If you meet the tax filing and income conditions on Worksheets A and B, you do not have to complete Section G to apply for Federal student aid.* Some states and colleges, however, require Section G information for their own aid programs. Check with your financial aid administrator and/or State Agency.

Age of your older parent **84.** [ ]

	STUDENT (& SPOUSE)	PARENT(S)
Cash, savings, and checking accounts	**77.** $ [ ].00	**85.** $ [ ].00
Other real estate and investments value *(Don't include the home.)*	**78.** $ [ ].00	**86.** $ [ ].00
Other real estate and investments debt *(Don't include the home.)*	**79.** $ [ ].00	**87.** $ [ ].00
Business value	**80.** $ [ ].00	**88.** $ [ ].00
Business debt	**81.** $ [ ].00	**89.** $ [ ].00
Investment farm value *(See Instructions, page 8.)* *(Don't include a family farm.)*	**82.** $ [ ].00	**90.** $ [ ].00
Investment farm debt *(See Instructions, page 8.)* *(Don't include a family farm.)*	**83.** $ [ ].00	**91.** $ [ ].00

SAMPLE

Healthcare Career Starter

Section H: Releases and Signatures

Page 4

92–103. What college(s) do you plan to attend in 1997–98?
(Note: The colleges you list below will have access to your application information. See Instructions, page 8.)

Housing codes	1—on-campus	3—with parent(s)
	2—off-campus	4—with relative(s) other than parent(s)

	Title IV School Code	College Name	College Street Address and City	State	Housing Code
XX.	0 5 4 3 2 1	EXAMPLE UNIVERSITY	14930 NORTH SOMEWHERE BLVD. ANYWHERE CITY	S T	XX. 2
92.					93.
94.					95.
96.					97.
98.					99.
100.					101.
102.					103.

104. The U.S. Department of Education will send information from this form to your state financial aid agency and the state agencies of the colleges listed above so they can consider you for state aid. Answer **"No"** if you don't want information released to the state. *(See Instructions, page 9 and "Deadlines for State Student Aid," page 10.)* .... 104. No ○ 2

105. Males not yet registered for Selective Service (SS): Do you want SS to register you? *(See Instructions, page 9.)* .... 105. Yes ○ 1

106–107. Read, Sign, and Date Below

All of the information provided by me or any other person on this form is true and complete to the best of my knowledge. I understand that this application is being filed jointly by all signatories. If asked by an authorized official, I agree to give proof of the information that I have given on this form. I realize that this proof may include a copy of my U.S. or state income tax return. I also realize that if I do not give proof when asked, the student may be denied aid.

Statement of Educational Purpose. I certify that I will use any Federal Title IV, HEA funds I receive during the award year covered by this application solely for expenses related to my attendance at the institution of higher education that determined or certified my eligibility for those funds.

Certification Statement on Overpayments and Defaults. I understand that I may not receive any Federal Title IV, HEA funds if I owe an overpayment on any Title IV educational grant or loan or am in default on a Title IV educational loan unless I have made satisfactory arrangements to repay or otherwise resolve the overpayment or default. I also understand that I must notify my school if I do owe an overpayment or am in default.

Everyone whose information is given on this form should sign below. The student (and at least one parent, if parental information is given) **must** sign below or this form will be returned unprocessed.

106. Signatures   *(Sign in the boxes below.)*

¹ Student

² Student's Spouse

³ Father/Stepfather

⁴ Mother/Stepmother

107. Date completed   Month Day   Year
1997 ○
1998 ○

Section I: Preparer's Use Only

For preparers other than student, spouse, and parent(s). Student, spouse, and parent(s), sign in question 106.

Preparer's name (last, first, MI)

Firm name

Firm or preparer's address (street, city, state, ZIP)

108. Employer identification number (EIN)

OR

109. Preparer's social security number

Certification: All of the information on this form is true and complete to the best of my knowledge.

110. Preparer's signature   Date

School Use Only

D/O ○   Title IV Code

FAA Signature

MDE Use Only
Do not write in this box   Special handle

MAKE SURE THAT YOU HAVE COMPLETED, DATED, AND SIGNED THIS APPLICATION.
Mail the original application (NOT A PHOTOCOPY) to: Federal Student Aid Programs, P.O. Box 4008, Mt. Vernon, IL 62864-8608

THE INSIDE TRACK

Who:	James Baker
What:	Radiologic technology student
Where:	Carti School of Radiation Therapy Technology, Little Rock, Arkansas

Insider's Advice

I was 24 when I went back to school, so I wasn't dependent on my parents, but I didn't have much money of my own either. I applied for financial aid as soon as I found out which school I was applying to. I knew I probably wouldn't get a grant because I worked part time and I didn't have any dependents. I thought the best chance I'd have was to get a low-interest loan. I received an unsubsidized Stafford loan.

Since I was working part time, I didn't need the whole amount they offered. I asked if I could take only what I needed, so I wouldn't owe so much money and interest after school. I figured out my school expenses and my living expenses, and my financial aid advisor and I came up with a reasonable borrowing amount. My advice is to do the same. Don't borrow more than you need and end up putting yourself into major debt. An unsubsidized loan gathers interest as long as you have it. I began paying the interest as I made a little extra money from work. This means my debt will be lower when I finish school.

Insider's Take on the Future

I want to get a good job as a radiologic technologist at a reputable hospital when I finish my certificate training. I'm not sure what I will do after that. My future is still pretty open to suggestion. I became interested in radiology after I had an accident that caused head trauma. I wanted to be able to understand the x-ray and be able to explain what I was looking at. Once I begin working and finally pay off my loan, I may go back to school, or who knows where I may end up.

CHAPTER 5

HOW TO LAND YOUR FIRST JOB

This chapter explains how to land your first job after your training program. First you'll learn how to conduct your job search, from researching the field to using classified ads, on-line resources, hotlines, job fairs, and industry publications. Then you'll find advice on how to write your resume and cover letter, and helpful tips on how to ace your interview. Next comes information on networking, including ways to make and maintain networking contacts. You'll also find comments from career counselors, employment recruiters, and workers who have advice on landing a job.

You can begin seeking employment while still in school, if you are not too far from graduation and any certification you need. There are many ways to conduct your job search, from searching want ads in the newspaper to sending out a slew of resumes. Read on for the latest information on how to land a great job in the healthcare field.

CONDUCTING YOUR JOB SEARCH

The more positions you apply for, the better your chances of landing a job. Major cities usually offer more employment opportunities than smaller towns or cities, so be aware that your location has a lot to do with job availability. Also be aware that most job applicants apply for a number of openings before they find employment.

Help-Wanted Ads

One way to search for a job is by reading the classified advertisements in your local newspapers, trade journals, and professional magazines. Trade journals and professional magazines are not only a good place to find advertisements, but also a useful source of information on current medical trends.

When you find openings that interest you, follow up on each ad by the method requested. You may be asked to phone or send a resume. Record the date of your follow-up, and if you don't hear from the employer within two or three weeks, place another call or send a polite note asking whether the job is still open.

An occupational assistant from San Francisco, California, explains how he got his job through a classified ad:

> I found my current job by answering a want ad in the *San Francisco Observer*. It was not the first job for which I tried to get an interview through the newspaper. The ad said to call, so I did, and I was given an interview date and time. I dressed up in a jacket and tie for the interview, and I must have impressed them. They interviewed five others for the job, but two weeks later I was hired. I had a 90-day probationary period, so if things didn't work out, either they or I could terminate the employment within that time.

Career Services

Most vocational schools, high schools, and colleges have a placement or career service center. If you are a student or a recent graduate, you should check these resources for job leads first. Many employers recruit employees from technical or trade schools and colleges. They may hold job fairs and conduct on-campus interviews with students.

Local and state employment services are another source of information for job openings. There are more than 2,700 such offices in the nation, and many employers automatically list their job openings at the local office. Whether you're looking for a job in private industry or with the state, these offices, which are affiliated with the federal employment service, are worth contacting. Private employment agencies will help you get a job if they think they can place you. Most employment agencies get paid by a company only if they place you in a job at that company, so you need to show the agency that you are a good prospect. Agency staff will help you prepare a resume if you need one, and they will contact employers they think might be interested in you. Some may require a small registration fee whether or not you get a job through them.

Computer placement services are the latest job search method. You send your resume or employment profile to a databank (computerized information file); when companies that subscribe to the service have a job to fill, they can call up a certain combination of qualifications on their computer system and quickly receive information on appropriate candidates. If you have access to the Internet, you might want to check out a few of these resources. See the section below, *On-line Resources,* for specific web addresses.

Temporary Agencies

Temporary work is a good way to get a handle on the job market. Many agencies specialize in placing people in short-term healthcare jobs. Nurses, nurse's aides, and medical technicians are among the types of workers most in demand. Temporary employment can increase your job skills, your knowledge of a particular field, and your chances of finding out about permanent positions. A temporary job also can lead to a permanent position.

On-line Resources

The Internet has become a great place to scout for jobs. Multiple career centers on the World Wide Web offer classified ads and jobs within specific careers for qualified applicants. For example, the website addresses http://www.careermosaic.com and http://www.jobweb.org offer numerous job listings in the healthcare field, from nurses to medical assistants. Use the search component of the Internet with the search words "jobs" and "health jobs."

Health magazine and newsgroup web pages, such as http://www.healthgate.com and http://www.medsearch.com, also advertise jobs. Some hospitals and companies also have web pages that list job openings, such as http://www.medctr.ucla.edu/ (UCLA Medical Center) and http://www.reidhosp.com (Reid Hospital and Health Care Services in Richmond, Indiana). Use the search component of the Internet with the search words "hospitals," "health," and "medical centers," or search the name of a particular hospital or medical center to see if it has a website listed. See the table of web addresses for more job-related websites.

Job Related Sites	
http://www.ajb.dnl.us	Over 1,800 state employers.
http://www.careermosaic.com	Jobs, company profiles, online job fairs.
http://www.hoovers.com	Company profiles.
http://intellimatch.com	Online resources and resume assistance.
http://jobbankusa.com	The largest list of job openings on the Internet.
http://www.monster.com	Over 55,000 jobs and resume assistance.
http://www.occ.com	Online resources, online job fairs, and career guidance.
http://jobsource.com	Job listings, company profiles, online resources, and resume assistance.
http://www.jobweb.com	Job listings, company profiles, and online resources.
http://www.careersite.com	Job listings and online resources.

Job Fairs

Most colleges and universities hold at least one job fair per year. Job fairs are not just for graduating seniors looking for employment; they also are useful for enhancing networking skills. You should attend job fairs in business attire and bring along at least ten copies of your resume.

Many companies also hold job fairs to hire employees. They often are advertised in your local newspaper's classified sections. Most job fairs take place about once a year.

Job Hotlines

Each city has its own job hotline monitored by the state employment agency. You can call your local employment agency for the phone number of the hotline that offers daily lists of jobs in your area. For a list of 5,000 job hotline numbers, check *The 1996 National Job Hotline Directory* in the reference department of your local library. Some local radio stations also offer job information and hotlines.

NETWORKING YOUR WAY INTO A JOB

Networking is a great way to find prospective career opportunities. It opens doors you never knew about and helps you find a job with the help of a reference, which is sometimes better than searching on your own. Many times employers will hire you based on a current employee's suggestion because the employer respects the employee who is recommending you. Do not leave networking out of your job search. Read on to find out why.

What Is Networking?

Networking means calling and talking with friends, acquaintances, and people you don't know about jobs in your area of interest and asking for advice and support. If you would like to work as a physical therapy assistant, get in touch with all the people you know who work in hospitals or private practices or who have friends or relatives in the field. Talk to your family, friends, counselors, former employers, and anyone else you can think of who may be aware of a suitable job opening. You may discover a job even before the job opening is advertised.

Make a list of everyone you know in the healthcare field. Send a friendly letter to everyone on the list. You may want to include your resume when writing to people who are in a position to help you, or you can call and ask if they'd mind if you sent it. Think about how you can begin making yourself more attractive, useful, and helpful to employers. Use your self-evaluation and your informal interviewing skills when you network with others.

You never know what opportunity someone will be able to find for you. Only about 20 to 30 percent of job vacancies are advertised; many employers look for employees by word of mouth. This is called the "hidden job market." In today's competitive climate, successful candidates must pursue all possible outlets. Networking is at least as important as visiting the career planning center at your school and checking help wanted ads. You want to gain as much exposure as possible.

Gaining Good Contacts

When establishing a network, you need to consider all possible living, breathing human resources: family, friends (including neighbors and parents of classmates), school personnel (teachers, counselors, alumni, administrators), previous employment contacts (employers, coworkers, customers, competitors), professionals (doctors, dentists, practicing professionals in your field), and community (business people, and members of clubs, associations, chambers of commerce, and religious groups). You also can use magazine articles, newspapers, or other general publicity to begin targeting people you would like to include in your network.

It is important not to overlook any possibilities. However, you shouldn't use a contact's name without permission when you contact a potential employer. Don't assume your friend will go out on a limb to recommend you. Once you have received the networking information, use your own ability to get the job. A registered nurse from Jackson, Mississippi, explains:

> I asked my uncle, who was a surgeon at a local hospital, if he knew of any openings around his hospital. I had been working for a nursing home and really wanted to get into a hospital where I might have more opportunity for promotion. He said he would get back to me, and when he did, he gave me the name of the nursing recruiter. He had talked her into giving me an interview before I even filled out an application. The interview was successful, and so is my career in nursing.

Making Contact

It's time to begin asking others for help. Contacting a whole list of people for favors can be nerve-racking. However, the key to succeeding as a networker and avoiding a major case of networking negativism lies in understanding that you aren't asking for a giant favor that creates a debt and gives others leverage over you. You are subtly empowering the other party while not asking for much in return.

When you contact someone, first identify yourself clearly. If someone referred you to this person, identify not only yourself but your referral source as well. Then explain your job objectives and how you'd like your contact to help you.

Your contacts' willingness to help you will depend largely on how your requests are couched. Keep your requests for help brief, conversational, and low-key. Be sincere.

- Ask contacts if it is a good time to talk for about 10 minutes, and then ask them to share any information they have about openings pertinent to your job goals.
- Say you don't expect an immediate answer, and ask if you can call them back or meet on a specific date.
- Use phrases such as "if I can make an appointment to talk," "if we can meet for a few minutes so that I might get your thoughts and opinions about some job-search ideas I've been thinking about," "if I can drop in on you at work for a few minutes and pick your brain," or "if I can get some advice on getting some exposure in the healthcare market."

Keep it light and pleasant, and to make it all easier, recite what you plan to say before you make that important call.

Last, but certainly not least, write a letter to thank your contacts for their time. Tell them you really appreciate their help and that you are grateful for their willingness to mention you to their colleagues. Thank them as well for any referrals they may have given you. Also let them know that you will keep them updated about what happens. Many contacts will be interested to know that their input helped you.

Expanding Your Contacts

Ask the people you contact for other referrals. Your contacts may call the referrals to prepare them for your call and to make sure they're willing to talk with you.

Don't be afraid to contact people directly, even if they are complete strangers. You are paying them a compliment by contacting them. People like to talk about themselves. And remember, everybody likes a good listener. You are empowering these people when you ask for their personal advice, information, and wisdom.

Organizing Your Contact List

You will need to keep track of your contacts. Keep their names on three-by-five-inch index cards, in a notebook or personal organizer, or in a computer database. Use a tracking system that is comfortable for you. Set up your network file to include the following contact information:

- Name of contact
- Address and telephone number
- How you met this person
- Occupation
- Date last contacted
- Conversation summary
- Names of referrals
- Date of thank-you letter
- Other comments

Maintaining Your Contacts

Keep in touch. Check in with your contacts every month to let them know how your job hunt is progressing. Keeping visible will generate further job leads. The key to faster success in your networking efforts is follow-up.

Unfortunately, the majority of follow-up calls aren't going to produce valuable new information or insights. But a timely follow-up call can jog your contact's short-term memory and get results.

In addition to writing thank-you notes, you can clip and send relevant articles or follow up on personal information shared in your conversation. Perhaps your contacts mentioned a ball game they went to or a type of music they like; if you mention this again, you're likely to stand out in their memory.

WRITING YOUR COVER LETTER

The first impression you make on an employer is likely to be on paper. Your written correspondence usually is what makes employers interested in giving you a personal interview. Your potential employer is likely to equate a clear, neat letter with good work habits and a sloppy one with bad work habits.

A cover letter is written to "inquire" about an open position. A good cover letter should be neat, clear, brief, and, most importantly, specific. It should be no more than three or four paragraphs long. You should send this letter to a specific person, either the personnel director or the person for whom you hope to work. If you don't know that person's name, call the company and ask to whom you should write.

Begin your letter by explaining why you are writing. Let the person know that you are inquiring about possible job openings at the company, that you are responding to an advertisement in a particular publication, or that someone recommended that you write. Your letter should introduce the information on your resume and call attention to your qualifications. Add information that shows you are suited for the job. Always thank the reader for his or her attention to your letter, and add that you look forward to hearing back soon. Use the following examples to help you draft a personalized cover letter.

Emily J. Small
135 Lariott Court ♦ Tampa, FL 12345

February 5, 1998

Gary Johnson
Personnel Department
St. Joseph's Hospital
P.O. Box 1565
Clearwater, FL 12345

Dear Mr. Johnson:

I am writing to inquire about openings for medical assistants in your hospital. I have read and heard many favorable things about your hospital, and I feel that this would be the perfect work environment for me. The fact that St. Joseph's Hospital is a small but rapidly growing hospital presents some intriguing challenges, and I am very interested in an available position.

I recently graduated from the medical technology assistant program at Med Tech Community College and received a certificate as a medical assistant. I have experience typing business correspondence and putting together statistical and financial reports, and I am familiar with many different types of forms, including inventory and tax forms. My typing speed is 65 wpm. I have experience with customer relations, including answering telephones, greeting clients, and answering questions the clients may have.

I have hands-on experience with all major office equipment, including word processors and photocopiers. I own a personal computer, so I have experience with a variety of word processing software, Lotus 1-2-3, and Microsoft Excel.

I always have been interested in helping people as well as working with computers. When I entered the medical assistant program, I learned that I am a hard worker as well as a caring individual. My training also taught me how to work under pressure while remaining organized to meet deadlines.

Enclosed is my resume, and I would be free to meet with you at your convenience. Also, I can arrange for you to speak with my references if you would like. Thank you for your attention to my letter. I can be reached at 111-555-9898 or at the address above. I look forward to hearing from you.

Sincerely,

Emily J. Small
Enc: Resume

James T. Anderson
6895 Peabody Ave.
Dallas, TX 45768

February 2, 1998

Elizabeth Townsend
Personnel Manager
St. Mary's General Hospital
P.O. Box 54G
Dallas, TX 45769

Dear Ms. Townsend:

I am writing in response to your ad in the Sunday, February 1, 1998, *Texas Journal and Constitution* newspaper. The ad stated that you are looking for someone with experience as a radiologic technologist. I am a recent graduate of Bryman College's radiologic technologist program with an associate degree, and I am looking for just this type of employment.

I have a good rapport with patients, doctors, and other technicians, but most importantly, I like being a radiologic technician and am completely dedicated to my work. I'll knock myself out to make sure a job is completed well, and I don't need constant supervision or constant pats on the back to keep me working hard.

If you need a radiologic technician who is good under pressure, experienced, and completely dedicated, I think we have something to talk about. I have the talent, the knowledge, and the skills needed to be a successful radiologic technician.

Enclosed is my resume, and I would be free to meet with you at your convenience. Thank you for your attention to my letter. I can be reached at 777-555-1323 or at the address above. I look forward to hearing from you.

Sincerely,

James T. Anderson
Enc: Resume

WRITING YOUR RESUME

The word *resume* originates from the French word *resumer*, meaning "to summarize," and that is exactly what you will do with your resume. Briefly outline your education, work experience, special abilities, and skills. A resume also may be called a personal profile or a personal data sheet. This summary can act as your introduction by mail, your calling card if you are applying in person, and as a convenient reference when you are filling out an application form or being interviewed. A resume is usually required for getting a job, and it can help you more than you think.

The purpose of a resume is to capture the interest of potential employers so they will call you for a personal interview. That means you want to highlight the following sections:

- Objective
- Education
- Work experience
- Employment history
- Special skills
- Related experience
- Personal qualifications

Preparing a self-inventory first will help you write a resume by pinpointing the items that show your ability to do the job or jobs in which you are interested. Select only those facts that point out your relevant skills and experiences. At the top of your resume, put your name, address, e-mail address, and phone number. Then decide which items will be most interesting to the employer you plan to contact.

Objective

Under your name and address you should state your job objective—your reason for contacting the employer. Describe briefly the type of position for which you are applying. Don't be too specific if you need to use the same resume several times. You may need to give a general career goal; then, in a cover letter, you can be more specific about the position you are seeking in the particular company you are contacting. However, if you have the flexibility of your own computer and printer, then it's best to tailor each resume for each position.

Educational Background

When listing your educational background, start with your most recent training and work backward. Employers want to know your highest qualifications at a glance. For each educational experience, include dates attended, name and location of school, and degree or certificate earned. If you have advanced degrees (college and beyond), it isn't necessary to include your high school education.

Work Experience

Every interested employer will and should check your educational background and employment history carefully. Employers do not want to hire people who have falsified their resume in any way. Make sure to list only past employers with whom you had positive experiences. If you don't have any related work experience yet, find some way to connect summer jobs, volunteer work, or part-time jobs to your current goals. If you were a manager at a restaurant, and you are now applying for a managerial position, it's appropriate to mention this job. Or you can highlight your interaction with customers to show your skill in working with the public.

Special Skills

You may wish to include another section called "Skills," "Related experience," or "Personal qualifications." Write down any skills such as typing, knowledge of software titles, knowledge of office equipment, supervisory experience, and any other skill you think may be useful in your future job.

Ways to Organize Your Resume

You can organize your resume in different ways to highlight specific areas of experience. Since some people have work experience and others do not, the different styles enable you to organize your resume in the most advantageous manner.

The Chronological Resume

The most common resume format is chronological—you summarize your work experience year by year.

Begin with your current or most recent employment and then work backward. For each job, list the name and location of the company for which you worked, the dates you were employed, and the position(s) you held. The order in which you present this information will depend on what you are trying to emphasize. If you want to call attention to the type or level of job you held, you should put the job title first. Be consistent. Summer employment or part-time work should be labeled as such, and you will need to specify the months in the dates of employment for positions you held for less than a year.

The Functional Resume

The functional resume emphasizes what you can do rather than what you have done. It is useful for people who have large gaps in their work history or who have relevant skills that would not be properly highlighted in a chronological listing of jobs. The functional resume concentrates on your qualifications—anything from familiarity with hospital procedures to organizational skills or managerial experience. You can mention specific jobs, but they are not the primary focus of this type of resume. This type of resume is useful if you have little work experience.

The Combination Resume

A combination of the chronological and functional resume may best highlight your skills. A combination resume allows you to present your skills as well as a chronological list of jobs you've held. You get the best of both resumes. This is an excellent choice if you have limited work experience and want to highlight specific skills.

Sample Chronological Resume

JEAN THOMPSON
1234 Third Street
Kansas City, MO 64131
816-246-4510   JeanT@aol.com

OBJECTIVE
To obtain a medical assistant position.

EDUCATION
Medical assistant certificate, June 1997 (12-week program)
Tad Technical Institute, 7910 Troost Ave., Kansas City, MO 64131
GPA: 3.95

Great Lions High School, Kansas City, MO 64130, June 1996
GPA: 3.98

WORK EXPERIENCE
Candy striper, nurse aide volunteer, 1995–1996
St. Mary's Hospital, Kansas City, MO 64130. Served meals and helped patients eat, dress, and bathe. Delivered messages and answered patient call bells. Completed daily filing and answered telephones. Inventoried, stored, and moved supplies.

Assistant evening manager, 1994-1995
King Seafood Restaurant, Kansas City, MO 64133. Waited on tables and greeted customers. Took over arranging staff schedule. Balanced register and deposited money. Learned how to order food and soft drinks. Managed personnel when manager was absent.

COMPUTER EXPERIENCE
Typing 65 wpm

Macintosh, IBM, Claris Works, Microsoft Word, WordPerfect, Lotus 1-2-3, E-mail

HONORS AND AWARDS
Student of the Year, 1997, Tad Technical College, Kansas City, MO

ACTIVITIES
Volunteer at Meltrice's Nursing Home in Wilmington, MO, and at local food shelters.

REFERENCES
References furnished from Tad Technical College, Career Planning and Placement Office, Griffin Hall, Kansas City, MO 64131; 816-555-1231

Sample Functional Resume

JACK WOODSON
1234 Second Ave.
Jackson, MS 10908
601-555-9876

OBJECTIVE: To obtain a career as a nursing assistant.

VOLUNTEER NURSING ASSISTANT

- Two years volunteer experience as nursing assistant in competitive hospital.
- Performed typical nursing assistant duties.
- Monitored patient status.
- Became familiar with radiologic technology by taking bone x-rays.

CLINIC ASSISTANT

- Assisted medical assistant with paperwork and filing.
- Ran basic errands and answered phones.

EDUCATION

- Associate degree in radiologic technology, June 1997
- University of Mississippi Medical Center, Jackson, Mississippi
  Major: Radiology
  GPA: 3.8/4.0

REFERENCES

References furnished by the Career Planning and Placement Center, University of Mississippi, Jackson, MS; 601-555-9876

Sample Combination Resume

Jennifer Perkins
1234 Obart St.
Orlando, FL 33054
407-555-7656

OBJECTIVE

To obtain a position as a dental assistant.

QUALIFICATIONS

Skilled dental assistant. Good rapport with dentists and patients. Specialty in periodontics. Expertise in all areas of general practice dentistry. Knowledgeable in office procedures. Devoted to patient education.

EDUCATION

College of Medicine and Dentistry
University of North Carolina, Chapel Hill, NC
Dental assistant certification, 1997

CLINICAL TRAINING

Administrative training includes:

- Scheduling and confirming appointments.
- Sending and receiving faxes.
- Making orders for supplies and materials.
- Patient relations.

Clinical training includes:

- Knowledge of instruments.
- Preparation of tray setup.
- Providing postoperative instruction to patients.
- Removing sutures and excess cement.

RELATED EXPERIENCE

Volunteer dental assistant, West Front Free Clinic, Orlando, 1/96-12/97, assisting father's practice after school.

- Greeted patients.
- Filed insurance forms and treatment records.
- Scheduled and confirmed appointments.
- Answered telephones.

REFERENCES

Available upon request.

> **Resume Writing Tips**
>
> - Be neat and organized.
> - Include ample white space.
> - Try to limit resume to one page, but do not crowd it. Go to two pages if necessary.
> - Use action verbs.
> - Be consistent in style.
> - Be positive and confident in your resume, but don't lie or embellish.
> - Don't be flashy or ostentatious—use white, cream, or gray paper.
> - Go to your local library or bookstore to read more sample resumes.

ACING YOUR INTERVIEW

The interview is the most important aspect of a job hunt because the impression you make on a prospective employer could be the reason you do or don't get the job. Interviewers are looking for specific qualities when they ask questions. Many people become nervous when attending an interview, but being well prepared can lessen your anxiety.

Information Interview

Arrange an *information interview* with someone who is in a position similar to the one you want. To make maximum use of the time that person is willing to spend with you, be sure to ask direct, pertinent questions and get complete information. This will enable you to make a better decision about whether to pursue a particular field. Here is a list of questions that will help you get the information you want in an information interview:

- Please give me a general description of the work you do.
- What is your typical workday like?
- What do you find most rewarding about your work?
- What are the toughest problems you encounter in your job?
- What are the frustrations in your work?
- What compromises are most difficult to make?
- If you could change your job in some way, what would it be?
- What educational degrees, licenses, or other credentials are required for entry and advancement in your kind of work? Which are preferred or most helpful?

- What trade/professional groups do you belong to, and which do you find most beneficial in your work? Do any of them assist students interested in entry-level positions in your field?
- What abilities, interests, values, and personality characteristics are important for effectiveness and satisfaction in your field?
- How do people usually learn about job openings in your field?
- What types of employers, other than your own, hire people to perform the type of work you do? Do you know of any that offer entry-level training programs or opportunities?
- If you were hiring someone for an entry-level position in your field, what would be the critical factors influencing your choice of one candidate over another?
- Is there anything else you think I would benefit from knowing about this field?

After an information interview, not only will you be more knowledgeable about your prospective position, but you also will gain interview experience, which may lessen the anxiety in your job interview.

Preparing for Your Interview

Preparation will enable you to be confident, overcome interviewing inexperience, and sell yourself and your qualifications. You should have your resume with you (although the company may already have it) as well as a personal inventory (a reference of possible answers to interview questions) to guide you as you describe your strengths and give examples to support your resume. One way to create a personal inventory is to write a short personal autobiography. Having a small autobiography handy will help you remember answers to the more challenging interview questions.

Research the company you're applying to so you feel more comfortable and can demonstrate genuine interest in the company during the interview. The public library is a good source for this kind of information, as are health publications. The idea is to converse knowledgeably about the company during the interview.

Dress for success. This may seem trivial, but you don't want to miss a job offer simply because of unprofessional attire. What you wear says a lot about your personality and attitude. Dress to show you are proud of yourself and your accomplishments. For men, a conservative suit with a white shirt and contrasting tie, well-shined shoes, and socks over the calf should be appropriate. For women, a jacket and skirt or dress in navy or black, neutral or sheer hose, simple pumps, and simple makeup are appropriate for most situations.

Allow sufficient time for the interview. It's likely you will be interviewing with more than one person during the interview cycle. You won't be at your best if you are worried about another appointment. It is a mistake to rush your interviewers because you have made a previous and conflicting commitment for the same day.

Arrive at the interview early. Arriving on time shows your respect for the interviewer and your professionalism. You do not want to be late. Allow extra travel time if you are unfamiliar with the employer's location.

Keep yourself in a positive frame of mind. Remember that you are there to discuss job-related topics, not your personal problems. If your interview begins on a "down beat," it may be difficult to turn the atmosphere around later. Turn the negative into a positive right away.

Go to the interview alone. If your spouse or a friend takes you to the interview, have that person wait for you elsewhere. A third party can be a negative distraction for both you and the interviewer.

Answering Tough Interview Questions

Employers tend to ask potential employees two kinds of questions: directive and open-ended. Directive questions attempt to gain, clarify, or verify factual information. Application forms are a series of directive questions. The open-ended question is an effort to draw out strengths and weaknesses. Some employers also may ask illegally discriminatory questions, probing for information that will lead them to draw conclusions based on stereotypes or assumptions about human behavior.

To deal effectively with all types of interview questions, you need to consider the employer's point of view. No matter what kind of question is asked, an employer really has only three questions:

1. Can you do the work? (Do you have the skills, competence, credentials, etc.?)
2. Will you do the work? (Do you have the motivation and stamina to produce?)
3. Can you get along with others, especially with me, your supervisor? (What are your interpersonal skills and key personality traits?)

A hospital employment manager from Jacksonville, Florida, describes a typical interview at her hospital:

> At our hospital, we give what is called a pattern interview, which is basically trying to find out how a person has acted in previous situations, whether at a job or in life situations so we can find out how they will react in future situations. For example, I would say, "Tell me the best type of supervisor that you have worked under" or "If you were caught in an error, how did you respond to that and solve the problem?" Most people will tell you exactly what they've done in the past, which is a good indication of what they will do in the future. We don't ask hypothetical questions. We want to know what they've done in reality.

When responding to questions, ask yourself: What is the underlying question? This is particularly important with open-ended and discriminatory questions. Accuracy and specificity are the keys to directive questions. The ability to understand yourself as a "product" and to express your strengths will help you answer open-ended questions more effectively.

Here are some questions frequently asked by employers:

- Tell me a little about yourself.
- Why should we hire you?
- What are your career objectives?
- If you could have the perfect position, what would it be?
- Do you have plans for continuing education?
- Why did you choose this career field?
- In what type of position are you most interested?
- What do you expect to be doing in five years?
- What is your previous work experience? What have you gained or learned from it?
- Why are you interested in our organization and in this particular opening?
- What salary do you expect to be earning now? In five years?
- Why did you choose your particular course of study?
- What do you consider to be your major weaknesses? Strengths?
- In what ways do you think you can make a contribution to our organization?
- What two or three accomplishments have given you the most satisfaction?

- Describe your most rewarding college experience.
- What have you learned from participation in extracurricular activities?
- Are you willing to relocate? Are you willing to travel?
- Do you think your grades are a good indication of your academic achievement?
- What have you done to show initiative and willingness to work?
- What types of books have you read? What journals do you subscribe to?
- What jobs have you enjoyed most? Least? Why?
- What do you think determines an employee's progress in a good company?
- What qualifications make you feel you will be successful in your field?

Asking Questions

Frequently, toward the close of the interview, the interviewer will provide the opportunity to ask questions. Don't ever say that you don't have any questions. This is your chance to set yourself apart from the competition. Prepare your questions in advance. Ask the most important questions first in case there is not enough time to ask all of them. Do not ask questions that might reveal a lack of research. It is inappropriate to ask about salary and benefits unless the employer is offering a position. Most employers do not want to discuss those issues until they are certain you are the right person for the job. Suitable questions include:

- What kind of career opportunities are currently available for my level of training and skills?
- Identify typical career paths based on past records. What is the realistic time frame for advancement?
- How is an employee evaluated and promoted? Is it company policy to promote from within?
- What is the retention rate for people in the position for which I am interviewing?
- Describe the typical first-year assignments.
- Tell me about your initial and future training programs.
- What are the challenging facets of the job?
- What are the opportunities for personal growth?
- What are the company's plans for future growth?
- What is the company's record of employment stability?
- What makes your practice different from your competitors?

- What are the company's strengths and weaknesses?
- How would you describe your company's personality and management style?

Follow-up Tactics

Send a courtesy letter to thank the interviewer for his or her time. Mention the time and date of the original interview and any important points discussed. Mention important qualifications that you may have omitted in the interview, and reiterate your interest in the job.

Don't get discouraged if a definite offer is not made at the interview, or if a specific salary is not discussed. The interviewer will usually communicate with her or his office staff or interview other applicants before making an offer. Generally, a decision is reached within a few weeks. If you do not hear from an employer within the time suggested during the interview, follow up with a telephone call. Show your commitment to their timetable. However, don't become a pest by calling every day for an answer.

THE INSIDE TRACK

Who:	Darren Denton
What:	Registered nurse
Where:	Not available
How long:	Over one year
How much:	$40,000 annually
Degree:	Associate degree in applied science in nursing
School:	East Tennessee University

Insider's Advice

I began my career as a certified nursing assistant (CNA), the basic entry-level position after I completed a brief class. Then I went back to school to become a licensed practical nurse (LPN). I went back to school to get my RN degree and worked full time as well. I just slipped into a higher position once I received my associate degree.

When I first applied for the CNA and the LPN jobs, I had to undergo a complete physical, including blood work. I also had to undergo drug testing. I submitted an application and underwent two interviews for the job as a LPN. I then had to submit a resume and another application to advance to the supervisory position.

The worst part of the process was the interviews. I think everyone should take a class in interview skills, possibly a required high school course. If you get the chance to take a class, do it. You probably will feel more secure during the interview.

Insider's Take on the Future

I have set some long-term goals for myself. These include going back to school. I plan to obtain my bachelor of science in nursing degree (BSN) and then my master's degree in extra corporeal perfusion therapy (ECPT) to become what is known as a perfusionist in the medical community. The perfusionist is the person who, among other things, runs the heart/lung bypass machine during open heart surgery.

CHAPTER | 6

HOW TO SUCCEED ONCE YOU'VE LANDED THE JOB

This chapter tells you how to thrive in your new career position. You'll learn about managing work relationships, fitting into the workplace culture, managing your time, finding a mentor, and promoting yourself from within the workplace. Also, you'll find interviews and helpful advice from employment supervisors and workers who are already in the field.

Landing the job is one thing. Keeping the job is another altogether. Completing a training program helps you understand work relationships, manage your time, and fit in, but when you are on the job, new challenges arise. Read on for the inside scoop on how to fit into the workplace culture, manage your time, and get along with your boss.

FITTING INTO THE WORKPLACE CULTURE

Many people are anxious on their first day of work, not only about whether they have the technical skill required to do the job, but also whether they will be accepted socially. The good news is that there are practical steps for fitting in and becoming a real member of the team.

Most of these steps are grounded in common sense. Good rules of thumb include:

- Be on time for work and meetings.
- Restrict your personal phone calls at work.

- Strike a balance of formality—be neither too familiar nor too standoffish.
- Follow the rules of good ethics: take responsibility for your actions, don't take credit for someone else's ideas, and own up to your mistakes.
- Concentrate on your work rather than on the impression you're making.
- If you don't know something, ask someone.
- Don't be offended if coworkers don't warmly include you on the first day.
- Help your coworkers if they need it.

How easily you adjust may depend on the type of job and the size of the company, as Mindy Reynolds, a chiropractic assistant from Kansas City, Missouri, explains:

> Being the newcomer can be hard, especially if the office is small and everyone has been there for a while. There were only six employees and two doctors at our practice when I first started. I just tried to be myself. I let everyone know that I had little experience other than training and that I would appreciate any help or advice that they had to offer. I was very open-minded and receptive to all the information everyone gave me. I also asked a lot of questions and wrote down everything I thought I needed to remember. You want to make sure you can get along with the others and carry on conversations about your job and life.

Many institutions give new employees an orientation to make sure they understand the daily routine, such as where to park, as well as policies and procedures. A general orientation may cover just about everything related to the company. In a department orientation, the resource person will work with new employees until they become familiar with their job. The length of such an orientation depends on employees' experience.

Many hospitals or large institutions give helpful classes in areas such as time management, getting along with coworkers, and dealing with ethical issues. Your supervisor can sign you up, or you can sign yourself up, depending on your company's policy. Classes like these are becoming more and more popular in our complex, competitive society.

How to Succeed Once You've Landed the Job

Managing Work Relationships

Managing work relationships becomes difficult when people develop problematic behaviors. Many healthcare organizations rely on their employees to get along; when treating patients, employees can't neglect their responsibilities simply because they don't want to work with someone else.

Managing your work relationships increases your own productivity. Learn about other departments and how other people's jobs rely on what you're doing. Exchanging information keeps your attitude positive, and it may help you learn about job openings in other departments. Building specific relationships with people in the workplace can create a more efficient environment for you and your coworkers.

Aimee Davidson, a dental assistant from Huntersville, North Carolina, explains the importance of managing work relationships in her office:

> As a dental assistant, I sit only about a foot and a half away from the doctor for almost eight hours a day. You want to make sure you can get along and that you can carry on a conversation without butting heads. You also want to make sure you know your job, so you won't slow the procedure down. You definitely have to be able to do several things at once and stay one step ahead of what the doctor wants. Doctors don't need someone who can't get along with them or who doesn't know the job well.

You need to manage your work relationships to foster a team approach. Here are some tips on building work relationships:

- Show integrity; demonstrate that what you say and do can be depended on.
- Be efficient so no one will have a problem with you.
- Show team spirit, especially if you are working with a team of people on a project.
- Have a good attitude and smile often.
- Complain with caution. Try every other avenue to resolve conflict before complaining to your boss. Like tattling, it could backfire.
- Don't get too personal or ask intrusive questions.

- Don't tell everyone your life story or let them know you're having a bad day, When people ask "How are you?" they generally expect to hear "Fine," not a report on your headache or kidney stones.
- Keep personal issues to yourself to prevent gossip. If you have a problem, go to your supervisor and discuss it. Don't expect the problem to work itself out, or you may be labeled the problem-maker.
- Don't expect everyone to be your best friend, or even helpful. Some people take their jobs more seriously than others' jobs, so don't expect everyone to take time out for you.
- Sincerely thank everyone who does help you.

If you do your job correctly and efficiently, mind your own business, and smile constantly, no one will be able to find fault. Cathy Holmes, a hospital unit secretary from Tampa, Florida, says:

> When I began in the hospital, most people were friendly and helpful. Don't be afraid to ask for help from others. Try to get along with the people you work with. Know that there are differences in personalities and lifestyles. Remember that you do not have to socialize outside the workplace. And don't gossip—you never know who may hear what you're saying.

Time Management Challenges

Efficiency is key to success in any office job. You need to manage your time wisely so you don't get bogged down by your workload or appear unable to handle your job. Many factors can make you inefficient on the job. Here's what to watch out for:

- **Disorganization.** Your inefficiency may spring from basic disorganization of workspace and time. If you often stay late or leave unfinished work, or feel there aren't enough hours in the day, disorganization may be to blame. Taking too many breaks, socializing, and procrastinating are often at the root of the problem. Lack of motivation can contribute as well. Change these habits and attitudes, and becoming organized will be easier.
- **Procrastination.** Procrastination may look like disorganization because in both cases you end up finishing tasks late. But the two problems aren't the same. Procrastination springs from one of three main sources: basic dislike

How to Succeed Once You've Landed the Job

of and lack of commitment to the task at hand, fear of not being able to measure up, or perfectionism.

- **Distraction from outside sources.** If you have too many distractions, you can't finish tasks or even leave work on time. Distractions mean a loss of concentration that can spell disaster for your workday. If you are a nursing assistant and you haven't finished your tasks before leaving, the assistants who come in after you are not going to be happy about having to do your leftover work. Too much socializing, a cluttered workspace, and a distracting flow of traffic by your station or desk can all affect your ability to concentrate.

- **Excessive on-the-job stress.** Some people can't stay awake, let alone work, unless they're surrounded by hubbub and beleaguered by nearly impossible-to-meet deadlines that constantly loom on the horizon. Other people are distracted by the soft tap-tap of keystrokes at the next desk. Ask yourself honestly whether you work best in a busy office surrounded by other people, in a quiet office, or alone. Often we have no choice: we've landed someplace and have to make the best of the environment. But on-the-job stress generally springs from two sources, so intertwined it's almost impossible to separate them: dealing with your boss and putting pressure on yourself.

Time Management Solutions

If you are going to become a nursing assistant or a medical assistant, you will have a variety of daily jobs. They may range from typing, filing, and scheduling appointments to making beds, delivering messages, helping patients eat or dress, and taking temperatures. Keeping up with your workload will help you be more efficient. Take on one task at a time, and you won't get bogged down or exhausted.

A surgical technologist notes:

> Time management is very important when you're getting ready for surgery, conducting surgery, and then cleaning up after surgery. There are times when I know the doctors don't need me, before and after surgery, so this is when I stock a room, check my supplies, get procedure instruments ready, and list what needs to be done. During surgery you have to be on the ball, aware of what instrument the doctor needs and what others around you are doing. You have to be on

top of your job and know others' jobs, or it could cost the patient his or her life. I never have time to stand around, unless it is break time.

Here are some effective techniques for overcoming the obstacles to good time management.

Create a To-Do List or Agenda

Schedule yourself to perform your duties in order of importance or time required. For example, if you are a medical assistant at a doctor's office and you have to file as well as type letters, decide which needs to be done right away, and do it first. Then cross it off your list.

Use Little Chunks of Time

Time leaks away in droplets, but it can be maximized in the same way. If you have five minutes before lunch and you just finished typing a report, there's no reason you can't start another, even if you won't finish it until after you get back. Or you can file one report. Or make a quick call to a patient, if that's on your list. Do anything but sit there staring at the clock. You'll be amazed at what you can accomplish. More importantly, making the most of your time will improve your attitude, giving you a sense of control over your day.

Reward Yourself

If you're working on a big task that takes several days, allow yourself a movie or dinner out after you've finished several small chunks. If it's a small task, allow yourself a snack at your desk. Reward yourself for your accomplishments; it's great motivation.

Eat Properly, Exercise, and Get Enough Sleep

Surprisingly often, boredom and lack of productivity at work stem from poor health habits, both on and off the job. Getting enough sleep at night is probably the single most important step you can take to improve your work performance. If you're tired, everything is harder, and all you can think about is quitting time. Skipping breakfast and eating junk food for lunch and dinner has a similar effect. A light, nutritious lunch, followed by a short walk, can greatly improve the quality of your workday afternoons.

Alternate Tasks to Add Variety

If you have some say in how you spend your time at work, add variety to your day by changing from one task to another rather than grimly working on one job until it's done. You shouldn't flip-flop compulsively, of course; but spending a little time typing, then filing, and then photocopying can stave off boredom and keep you from watching the clock.

Take Mini-Breaks

Sitting in one place, in one position, for long periods can be stultifying. But suppose you've taken on a one-task job and don't have the luxury of moving about or alternating tasks. Taking unobtrusive mini-breaks will not only alleviate body strain but aid relaxation. Here are some simple mini-breaks:

- Stand up and stretch a moment, then sit back down.
- Yawn and blink (these also help release tension and lubricate eyes).
- Massage your hands and fingers or cover your eyes with your palms.
- Do deep breathing exercises in your seat.
- Do isometric exercises, such as calf flexes, ankle twirls, stomach tightening and relaxation, gentle shoulder shrugs, and head-rolling.
- Stretch while remaining seated; clasp your hands behind your head and pull your shoulders way back (this is called the executive stretch).
- If you're allowed, get coffee or, better yet, juice or a healthy snack, and bring it back to your desk.
- Visit the bathroom once between breaks. Not even the strictest boss can fault you for that.

Rearrange Your Workstation

If you find yourself distracted by others—either because people tend to stop at your desk to chat or because they bump into your desk as they pass—it's best to reposition your workstation, if you're allowed to do so. You may want to turn so that you face a wall or window, or at least so you aren't facing into oncoming traffic.

Dealing With Your Boss

There are abusive bosses, and there are unbearable work environments. If you have examined your heart and have come to the conclusion that it really isn't just you, that in fact you're working for an abusive boss, you have three options:

1. First, find another job, then quit.
2. Fight, but expect you may have to pay a heavy price unless you have a good union.
3. Grin and bear it, meditate, or see a psychologist.

Not all bosses are abusive; some have a generally benign or at least neutral attitude toward their workers. But they operate under constant pressure, and that pressure is very likely to spill over onto you. Here are keys to resisting pressure from your supervisors:

- Remember that you have a life outside work.
- Set limits, even with your boss (at least if you have a reasonable boss).
- Learn physical relaxation techniques.

Internal Pressure

Often, the greatest pressure we have to bear is that which we put on ourselves. Some of it is necessary or we'd never get anything done, but it can reach bullying proportions if we let it. Following are three ways to relieve unreasonable pressure from within:

- Weed out perfectionism—care more about overall excellence than minor details.
- Care more about the quality of your work than about what others (including your boss) think of you.
- Be nice to yourself.

Finding a Mentor

One of your best resources at work is a good mentor. Some institutions call them resource persons. A mentor or resource person can help you greatly while you learn about your new job, get acquainted with your new building, and begin to adjust to your work surroundings. He or she also may teach you things about your job that you didn't learn in school.

Ronald Shane, an optometrist from Pennsylvania, describes his mentor:

> I am most grateful that the chief of the eye department at Giselle became my mentor and good friend. I will always be indebted to Dr. Richard Appell for the knowledge he has given me, as well as his guidance and friendship. He has changed my ideas about what optometry should be. I graduated from optometry school knowing a great deal about the eye but having no concept of what "vision" is. Dr. Appell showed me the difference between acuity and vision.

How to Succeed Once You've Landed the Job

> **Success Tips**
> - Make an effort to show up for work on time, all the time.
> - Show enthusiasm for new projects.
> - Smile and greet your supervisors when you meet them in the hall.
> - Be honest and don't gossip.
> - Don't be afraid to ask for help, and don't automatically think you know everything.
> - Keep a positive attitude to create a positive atmosphere.

Promoting Yourself

Many times in your career you'll have chances to promote yourself to a higher-level position or better hours. Before you ask for a promotion, show your employer or supervisor that you have dedicated yourself to your current position, you've performed well, your attendance is satisfactory, you've been cooperative and flexible, and you have gained the necessary training.

Hospitals usually hire entry-level workers for a contract position. You may be hired as a nurse's aid and required to keep that position for six months before requesting a promotion or schedule change. You should only accept the job if you can commit to these terms. A nursing recruiter from Athens, Georgia, explains:

> We tell applicants, "These are the hours of this position. Is there anything that would prevent you from working these hours?" We've got to know if the person's going to be able to work the hours. Some people will say they want days but they'll take nights. Well, we try not to do that because when you're hired into a night position, you're committed to that, and a lot of times, those people start applying right away to change to days. You can't do that. Don't take the job just to get your foot in the door.

After six months you are eligible to transfer if you have the qualifications and if your employment record is clean. You will need to fill out a job transfer request form explaining to your supervisor and others when and why you wish to transfer. You won't get promoted if you have performance or attendance problems.

Private practices and group practices hire different numbers of staff and have different work policies. You may be promoted as soon as you receive the training needed for a promotion, if the physician feels you can do the work. Here it is up to the employer; in hospitals, promotions follow more formal guidelines.

ACHIEVE SUCCESS

Once you've landed the job you've worked so hard to get, do your best to make it worth your time and energy. Put your best foot forward, and prove to your boss that you appreciate the chance to succeed. Form friendly relationships with coworkers, sharing ideas and common interests. Come to work on time, be efficient, and, even when you're having a bad day, smile and don't take it out on someone else.

Take classes in time management or work relationships if you need them. Find people in your work environment to take you under their wing. Promote yourself after you've proved your capabilities in a probationary period. Show everyone your best, and you will succeed and move on to greater opportunities and higher levels of pay.

THE INSIDE TRACK

Who:	Catherine A. Holmes
What:	Unit secretary II, surgery scheduling coordinator
Where:	University Community Hospital, Tampa, Florida
How long:	11 years
How much:	$21,000–$24,000 annually
Degree:	Computer terminal operator certificate (comparable to a medical assistant certificate)
School:	American Business Institute

Insider's Advice

Never stop learning. My willingness to learn new tasks helped me promote myself within my job area. I cross-trained for other positions and met managers in those areas. This broadened my contacts and demonstrated my abilities and worth. If you prove to your supervisors that you want to be successful at the job you have and want to learn more about other positions as well, your supervisors will eventually respond to that and move you up and around.

Insider's Take on the Future

I always wanted to be a nurse, since I was a child. I always wanted to help people and feel that my help really made a difference. I like the fact that there are so many different types of nursing jobs and a need for nurses almost everywhere you may travel. I am currently enrolled in a two-year associate degree in nursing program. However, I hope eventually to receive my bachelor of science in nursing degree (BSN) and possibly take management courses as well. I hope in five years to be working as an RN.

APPENDIX A

PROFESSIONAL ASSOCIATIONS

Here are some associations, according to your field of expertise, that you can contact for further information. Also included is contact information for accrediting organizations, internships, placement services, and scholarships in the healthcare field.

Dental Assistant

American Dental Association
211 E. Chicago Ave., Suite 1814
Chicago, IL 60611
American Dental Assistants Association
203 N. Lasalle, Suite 1320
Chicago, IL 60601-1225

Medical Assistant

American Association of Medical Assistants
20 North Wacker Dr., Suite 1575
Chicago, IL 60068-5765
312-424-3100

American Society of Pediatric Medical
Assistants
2124 S. Austin Blvd.
Cicero, IL 60650

Registered Medical Assistants of
America, Medical Technologists
710 Higgins Rd.
Park Ridge, IL 60068-5765
708-823-5169

Nursing Aide and Assistant

American Academy of Ambulatory
Nursing Administrators
N. Woodbury Rd., Box 56
Pitman, NJ 08071

American Academy of Nurse
Practitioners
179 Princeton Blvd.
Lowell, MA 08151

American Assembly for Men in Nursing
c/o College of Nursing, Rush University
600 S. Paulina, 474-H
Chicago, IL 60612

American Association for Critical Care
Nurses
One Civic Plaza
Newport Beach, CA 92660

American Association of Colleges of
Nursing
1 Dupont Circle, Suite 530
Washington, DC 20036

American Association of Nurse
Anesthetists
216 Higgins Rd.
Park Ridge, IL 60068

American Association of Nursing
Assistants
145 East 84th St.
New York, NY 10028

American Indian/Alaska Native Nurses
Association, Inc.
P.O. Box 3908
Lawrence, KS 66040

American Nurses Association
2420 Pershing Rd.
Kansas City, MO 64108

American Nursing Assistant's
Association
P.O. Box 103
Ottawa, KS 66067

American Society of Plastic and
Reconstructive Surgical Nurses, Inc.
N. Woodbury Rd., Box 56
Pitman, NJ 08071

Association of Operating Room Nurses,
Inc.
10170 East Mississippi Ave.
Denver, CO 80231

Professional Associations

Association of Pediatric Oncology
Nurses
Pacific Medical Center, P.O. Box 7999
San Francisco, CA 94120

Association of Rehabilitation Nurses
2506 Gross Point Rd.
Evanston, IL 60201

Canadian Nurses' Association
50 The Driveway
Ottawa, Ontario, Canada K2P1E2

Dermatology Nurses' Association North
Woodbury Rd., Box 56
Pitman, NJ 08071

Emergency Department Nurses'
Association
666 North Lake Shore Dr., Suite 1131
Chicago, IL 60611

National Association for Practical Nurse
Education and Service, Inc.
254 West 49th St.
New York, NY 10001

National Association of Hispanic Nurses
4359 Stockdale
San Antonio, TX 78233

National Association of Nurse Recruiters
111 E. Wacker Dr., Suite 600
Chicago, IL 60601

National Association of School Nurses,
Inc.
7706 John Hancock Ln.
Dayton, OH 45459

National Black Nurses' Association, Inc.
P.O. Box 18358
Boston, MA 02118

National League for Nursing
350 Hudson St.
New York, NY 10019

National Male Nurse Association
23309 State St.
Saginaw, MI 48602

National Student Nurse Association
Box 1211
Waterville, ME 04901

Physical Therapist Assistant
American Academy of Physical
Medicine and Rehabilitation
122 South Michigan Ave., Suite 1300
Chicago, IL 60603
312-922-9366

American Association for Rehabilitation
Therapy
P.O. Box 93
North Little Rock, AR 72115

American Physical Therapy Association
1111 North Fairfax St.
Alexandria, VA 22314-1488

American Association for Rehabilitation Therapy
P.O. Box 93
North Little Rock, AR 72115

National Rehabilitation Association
633 South Washington St.
Alexandria, VA 22314
703-715-9090

Radiologic Technologist

American Healthcare Radiology Administrators
111 Boston Post Rd., Suite 215
P.O. Box 334
Sudbury, MA 01776

American Radiological Nurses Association
502 Forest Court
Carrboro, NC 27510

American Registry of Diagnostic Medical Sonographers
600 Jefferson Plaza
Rockville, MD 20852-1150

American Registry of Radiologic Technologists
1255 Northland Dr.
Mendota Heights, MN 55120
612-687-0048

American Society of Radiologic Technologists
15000 Central Ave. SE
Albuquerque, NM 87123-3917

American Society of Radiologic Technologists
55 East Jackson Blvd.
Chicago, IL 60604

American Society of Radiologic Technologists
Job Referral Service
15000 Central Ave. SE
Albuquerque, NM 87123
505-298-4500

Joint Review Committee on Education in Diagnostic Medical Sonography
7108 S. Alton Way, Building C
Englewood, CO 80112

Joint Review Committee on Education in Radiologic Technology
20 N. Wacker St.
Chicago, IL 60606-2901

Radiological Society of North America
2021 Spring Rd., Suite 600
Oak Brook, IL 60521
708-571-2670

Society of Diagnostic Medical Sonographers
12770 Coit Rd., Suite 508
Dallas, TX 75251

Surgical Technologist

Accreditation Review Committee on Education in Surgical Technology
7108-C S. Alton Way
Englewood, CO 80112
303-694-9262

American Association of Surgeon Assistants
1600 Wilson Blvd., Suite 905
Arlington, VA 22209
703-525-1191

Association of Surgical Technologists
7108-C S. Alton Way
Englewood, CO 80112
303-694-9130

Liaison Council on Certification for the Surgical Technologist
7108-C S. Alton Way
Englewood, CO 80112
303-694-9264

General

American Health Care Association
1201 L St. NW
Washington, DC 20005-4014

American Hospital Association
840 N. Lake Shore Dr.
Chicago, IL 60611

American Public Health Association
1015 15th St. NW
Washington, DC 20005

Association for the Care of Children's Health
3615 Wisconsin Ave. NW
Washington, DC 20016

Department of Health and Human Services
200 Independence Ave., SW
Washington, DC 20201
202-245-6296

National Association of Health Career Schools
9570 West Pico Blvd., Suite 200
Los Angeles, CA 90035

National Council on the Aging
Division of the Foundation for Hospice and Homecare
519 C St. NE
Washington, DC 20002

National Rural Health Association
301 East Armour Blvd., Suite 420
Kansas City, MO 64111
816-756-3140

ACCREDITING ORGANIZATIONS

Accrediting Bureau of Health Education Schools
2700 South Quincy St., Suite 210
Arlington, VA 22206
703-998-1200

Commission on Accreditation of Allied
Health Education Programs
515 North State St., Suite 7530
Chicago, IL 60610
312-464-4623

Department of Allied Health Education
and Accreditation
American Medical Association
515 North State St.
Chicago, IL 60610
312-464-4660

INTERNSHIPS

Action AIDS
1216 Arch St.
Philadelphia, PA 19107
215-981-0088

American Cancer Society Internships
1599 Clifton Rd. NE
Atlanta, GA 30329

American National Red Cross
431 18th St. NW
Washington, DC 20006

American Nursing Assistants
Association
P.O. Box 103
Ottawa, KS 66067

March of Dimes Birth Defects
Foundation
1275 Mamaroneck Ave.
White Plains, NY 10605

Leukemia Society of America
600 Third Ave.
New York, NY 10016

PLACEMENT SERVICES

American Managed Care & Review
Association
1227 25th St. NW, #610
Washington, DC 20037
202-728-0506

American Public Health Association Job
Placement Service
1015 15th St. NW
Washington, DC 20005
202-789-5600

American School Health Association
Placement Service
P.O. Box 708
Kent, OH 44240
216-245-6296

National Association of Personnel
Services
3133 Mt. Vernon Ave.
Alexandria, VA 22305

National Association of Temporary
Services
119 S. Saint Asaph St.
Alexandria, VA 22314

Professional Associations

SCHOLARSHIPS

American Technological Scholarships
710 Higgins Rd.
Park Ridge, IL 60068

Dental Assisting Scholarship Program
ADA Endowment Fund and Assistance
211 East Chicago Ave.
Chicago, IL 60611

Maxine Williams Scholarships
American Association of Medical
Assistants Endowment
20 N. Wacker Dr., Suite 1575
Chicago, IL 60606

Nurse Education Scholarships
American Association of Homes for the Aging
901 E. St. NW, Suite 500
Washington, DC 20004-2037

MILITARY AND TRAVEL HEALTHCARE CAREERS

Department of the Air Force
Headquarters
U.S. Air Force Recruiting Service (ATC)
Randolph Air Force Base, TX 78150-5421

Department of the Army, Headquarters,
U.S. Army Recruiting Command
Fort Sheridan, IL 60037-6000

Department of the Navy, Navy
Recruiting Command
4015 Wilson Blvd.
Arlington, VA 22203-1911

Peace Corps
806 Connecticut Ave. NW
Washington, DC 20525

Project HOPE
Health Sciences Education Center,
Carter Hall
Millwood, VA 22646

American National Red Cross, National
Headquarters
17 and D Sts. NAW
Washington, DC 20006

U.S. Public Health Service
Department of Health and Human
Services
5600 Fishers Lane, Rm. 17-74
Rockville, MD 20757

World Health Organization
(Pan American Health Organization)
525 23 St. NW
Washington, DC 20037

DIRECTORIES

AHA Guide to the Health Care Field
American Hospital Association
P.O. Box 92683
Chicago, IL 60675-2683
800-242-2626
Hospitals, clinics, and other healthcare organizations.

Allied Health Education Directory
American Medical Association
P.O. Box 2964
Milwaukee, WI 53201-2964

American Association of Homes and Services for the Aging
1129 20th St. NW, Suite 400
Washington, DC 20036
202-296-5960
The AAHSA publishes numerous resources in the field of aging services.

American Group Practice Association
1422 Duke St.
Alexandria, VA 22314
703-838-0033
The AGPA publishes a directory of physicians' private medical practices, as well as educational materials and special reports.

Biliam's Hospital Blue Book
2100 Powers Ferry Rd.
Atlanta, GA 30339
404-955-5656
Hospitals.

Blue Book Digest of HMOs
National Association of Employers on Health Care Action
P.O. Box 220
Key Biscayne, FL 33149
305-361-2810
Health maintenance organizations.

Case Management Resource Guide
Center for Consumer Healthcare Information
1821 East Dyer Rd.
Santa Ana, CA 92705
714-752-2335
Health care facilities, adult daycare, cancer centers, and more.

Directory of Adult Daycare in America
National Institute on Adult Daycare
600 Maryland Ave., SW, West Wing 100
Washington, DC 20024
202-479-1200
Adult daycare centers and state associations.

Federation of American Health Systems Directory
1405 N. Pierce St., Suite 311
Little Rock, AR 72207
501-661-9555
Healthcare facilities nationwide.

Professional Associations

Hospital Phone Book U.S. Directory Service
655 NW 128th St.
Miami, FL 33168
305-769-1700
Hospitals.

Medical and Health Information Directory
Gale Research Company
Book Tower
Detroit, MI 48226
800-877-4253
Medical associations, schools, federal agencies, and more.

APPENDIX B

ADDITIONAL RESOURCES

Now that you've been through this entire book, you should have a good idea of what steps you need to take to begin a career in the healthcare field. This appendix offers a list of additional literature that will give you more specific advice on areas with which you feel you need help.

Colleges

Peterson's Guide to Two-Year Colleges 1998: The Only Guide to More Than 1,500 Community and Junior Colleges. Princeton, NJ: Peterson's. 1997.

The College Board, *The College Handbook 1998.* 35th Ed. New York: College Entrance Examination Board. 1997.

The Princeton Review, *The Complete Book of Colleges 1998.* New York: Random House, The Princeton Review. 1997.

Cover Letters

Beatty, Richard H., *The Perfect Cover Letter.* 2nd Ed. New York: John Wiley & Sons. 1997.

Besson, Taunee, *The Wall Street Journal National Business Employment Weekly: Cover Letters.* 2nd Ed. New York: John Wiley & Sons. 1996.

Marler, Patty and Jan Bailey Mattia, *Cover Letters Made Easy*. Lincolnwood, Illinois: VGM Career Horizons. 1996.

Financial Aid

Chany, Kalman A. and Geoff Martz, *Student Advantage Guide to Paying for College 1997 Edition*. New York: Random House, The Princeton Review. 1997.

College School Service, *College Costs & Financial Aid Handbook*. 18th Ed. New York: The College Entrance Examination Board. 1998.

Davis, Kristen, *Financing College: How to use Savings, Financial Aid, Scholarships, and Loans to Afford the School of Your Choice*. Washington, D.C.: Random House, Kiplinger. 1996.

Some previous edition financial aid guides are available at your local library.

Internships

Hamadeh, Samer and Mark Oldham, *America's Top Internships 1997*. 3rd Ed. New York: Random House, The Princeton Review. 1996.

Srinivasan, Kalpana and the *Yale Daily News*, *The Yale Daily News Guide to Internships 1998 Edition*. New York: Simon & Schuster. 1997.

Some previous edition internship guides are available at your local library.

Interviews

Bloch, Deborah P., Ph.D., *How to Have A Winning Interview*. Illinois: VGM Career Horizons. 1996.

Fry, Ron, *101 Great Answers to the Toughest Interview Questions*. 3rd Ed. Franklin Lakes, New Jersey: Book-Mart Press. 1996.

Kennedy, Joyce Lain, *Job Interviews for Dummies*. Foster City, CA: IDG Books. 1996.

Additional Resources

General Job Hunting

Bernstein, Sara T., and Kathleen M. Savage, Eds., *Vocational Careers Sourcebook.* New York: Gale Research, International Thompson Pub, 1996.

Bureau of Labor Statistics *Dictionary of Occupational Titles.* 4th Ed. Vol. 1, 2. Bureau of Labor Statistics. 1991.
Bureau of Labor Statistics. *Occupational Outlook Handbook 1996–1997.*

Cubbage, Sue A. and Marcia P. Williams, *The 1996 National Job Hotline Directory.* New York: McGraw-Hill. 1996.

Sunshine, Linda and John W. Wright, *The Best Hospitals in America.* Gale Research Inc.: Thompson Publishing. 1995.

Networking

National Business Employment Weekly, Networking: Insider's Strategies for Tapping the Hidden Market Where Most Jobs are Found. New York: John Wiley & Sons, 1994.

Office Politics

Bell, Arthur and Smith, Dayle M., *Winning With Difficult People.* New York: Barron's Educational Series, 1991.

Bramson, Robert M., Ph.D., *Coping With Difficult People.* New York: Anchor Press, 1981.

Felder, Leonard, *Does Someone at Work Treat You Badly?* New York: Berkeley Books, 1993.

Resumes

Adams Resume Almanac & Disc. Holbrook, Massachusetts: Adams Media Corporation. 1996.

Haft, Timothy D., *Trashproof Resumes: Your Guide to Cracking the Job Market.* Princeton, NJ: Princeton Review, 1995.

The Guide to Basic Resume Writing. Chicago: VGM Career Horizons, NTC Publishing Group, 1991.

Scholarship Guides

Cassidy, Daniel J., *The Scholarship Book: The Complete Guide to Private-Sector Scholarships, Grants, and Loans for Undergraduates.* Englewood Cliffs, NJ: Prentice Hall. 1996.

Ragins, Marianne, *Winning Scholarships for College: An Insider's Guide.* New York: Henry Holt & Co. 1994.

Scholarships, Grants & Prizes: Guide to College Financial Aid From Private Sources. Princeton, NJ: Peterson's. 1998.

Schwartz, John, *College Scholarships and Financial Aid.* New York: Simon & Schuster, Macmillan. 1995.

Scholarships 1998. New York: Simon & Schuster, Kaplan. 1997.

Some previous edition scholarships guides are available at your local library.

Studying

Coman, Marcia J. and Kathy L Heavers, *How to Improve Your Study Skills.* 2nd Ed. Lincolnwood, Illinois: NTC Publishing. 1998.

Fry, Ron, *Ron Fry's How to Study Program.* 4th Ed. New Jersey: Career Press. 1996.

Wood, Gail. *How To Study.* New York: LearningExpress. 1998.

Test Help

Andujo, Emily, RDH, BS, MS, *Dental Assistant Prep: Program Review and Exam Preparation.* Stamford, Connecticut: Appleton & Lange. 1996.

ACT: Powerful Strategies to Help You Score Higher: 1998 Ed. Kaplan. New York: Simon & Schuster. 1997.

Additional Resources

EMT-Basic Exam. New York: LearningExpress. 1997.

Gooding, Marion F., *Nursing School and Allied Health Entrance Exams.* 14th Ed. New York: ARCO Publishing. 1997.

Home Health Aide Exam. New York: LearningExpress. 1997.

Katyman, John and Adam Robinson, *Cracking the SAT & PSAT 1998 Edition.* New York: Random House, The Princeton Review. 1997.

Nursing Assistant Exam. New York: LearningExpress. 1997.

MASTER THE BASICS ... FAST!
WITH THE EXCLUSIVE LEARNINGEXPRESS ADVANTAGE

These books are for you if need to improve your basic skills to move ahead, either at work or in the classroom.
- Become a Better Student — *Quickly*
- Become a More Marketable Employee — *Fast*
- Get a Better Job — *Now*

Specifically Designed for Classroom Learning OR Independent Home Study!
- 20 easy-to-follow lessons build confidence and skill FAST
- Focus on real-world skills — what you REALLY need to succeed
- Dozens of exercises, hundreds of practical tips, and easy-to-implement steps to SUCCESS

___ READ BETTER, REMEMBER MORE	Item #060-9	___ HOW TO STUDY	Item# 084-6
___ IMPROVE YOUR WRITING FOR WORK	Item #061-7	___ PRACTICAL SPELLING	Item #083-8
___ GRAMMAR ESSENTIALS	Item #062-5	___ PRACTICAL VOCABULARY	Item #082-X
___ THE SECRETS OF TAKING ANY TEST	Item #071-4	___ MATH ESSENTIALS	Item #094-3

SPECIFICATIONS: 7 x 10 • 208 PAGES • $13.95 EACH (PAPERBACK)

  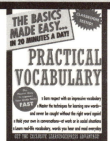 

ORDER THE BASICS MADE EASY YOU NEED TODAY:

Fill in the quantities beside each book and mail your check or money order*
for the amount indicated (please include $6.95 postage & handling
for the first book and $1.00 for each additional book) to:

LearningExpress, Dept. A040, 20 Academy Street, Norwalk, CT 06850

Or call, TOLL-FREE: **1-888-551-JOBS**, Dept. A040 to place a credit card order.

Also available in your local bookstores

Please allow at least 2-4 weeks for delivery. Prices subject to change without notice.   *NY, CT, & MD residents add appropriate sales tax

LEARNINGEXPRESS®
An Affiliate Company of Random House, Inc.

LearningExpress

At Last—
Test Preparation that *Really* Works

Improve Your Scores with the Exclusive LearningExpress Advantage!

Competition for top jobs is tough. You need all the advantages you can get. That's why LearningExpress has created easy-to-use test prep and career guides, many **customized** specifically for the high-demand jobs in your city and state.

Only LearningExpress gives:

➤ Exclusive practice exams based on official tests given in specific cities and states
➤ Hundreds of sample questions with answers & explanations by experts
➤ Key contacts, salaries & application procedures for individual cities

Plus:

➤ Unique LearningExpress Exam Planners
➤ Critical skill-building exercises in reading comprehension, math, and other commonly tested areas
➤ Detailed career information, including college programs for specific jobs, requirements and qualifications, comprehensive job descriptions, and much more

> **Thousands of Satisfied Customers Can't be Wrong:**
>
> "It's like having the test in advance."
> —Ms. J. Kennedy
>
> "Better than the $200 6-week study courses being offered. After studying from dozens of books I would choose yours over any of the other companies."
> —Mr. S. Frosh
>
> "Best test-prep book I've used."
> —Mr. H. Hernandez

Don't Delay!

To order any of these titles, fill in the quantities beside each book on the order form and mail your check/money order for the full amount* (please include $6.95 postage/handling for the first book and $1.00 for each additional book) to:

LearningExpress
Dept. A040
20 Academy Street
Norwalk, CT 06850

Or Call, TOLL-FREE:
1-888-551-JOBS, Dept. A040
to place a credit card order

LearningExpress books are also available in your local bookstore.

Please allow at least 2-4 weeks for delivery. Prices subject to change without notice.   *NY, MD, & CT residents add appropriate sales tax*

Order Form

CALIFORNIA EXAMS
- ___ @ $35.00 CA Police Officer
- ___ @ $35.00 CA State Police
- ___ @ $35.00 CA Corrections Officer
- ___ @ $20.00 CA Law Enforcement Career Guide
- ___ @ $35.00 CA Firefighter
- ___ @ $30.00 CA Postal Worker
- ___ @ $35.00 CA Allied Health

NEW JERSEY EXAMS
- ___ @ $35.00 NJ Police Officer
- ___ @ $35.00 NJ State Police
- ___ @ $35.00 NJ Corrections Officer
- ___ @ $20.00 NJ Law Enforcement Career Guide
- ___ @ $35.00 NJ Firefighter
- ___ @ $30.00 NJ Postal Worker
- ___ @ $35.00 NJ Allied Health

TEXAS EXAMS
- ___ @ $35.00 TX Police Officer
- ___ @ $30.00 TX State Police
- ___ @ $35.00 TX Corrections Officer
- ___ @ $20.00 TX Law Enforcement Career Guide
- ___ @ $35.00 TX Firefighter
- ___ @ $30.00 TX Postal Worker
- ___ @ $32.50 TX Allied Health

NEW YORK EXAMS
- ___ @ $30.00 NYC/Nassau County Police Officer
- ___ @ $30.00 Suffolk County Police Officer
- ___ @ $30.00 New York City Firefighter
- ___ @ $35.00 NY State Police
- ___ @ $35.00 NY Corrections Officer
- ___ @ $20.00 NY Law Enforcement Career Guide
- ___ @ $35.00 NY Firefighter
- ___ @ $30.00 NY Postal Worker
- ___ @ $35.00 NY Allied Health
- ___ @ $30.00 NY Postal Worker

MASSACHUSETTS EXAMS
- ___ @ $30.00 MA Police Officer
- ___ @ $30.00 MA State Police Exam
- ___ @ $30.00 MA Allied Health

FLORIDA EXAMS
- ___ @ $35.00 FL Police Officer
- ___ @ $35.00 FL Corrections Officer
- ___ @ $20.00 FL Law Enforcement Career Guide
- ___ @ $30.00 FL Postal Worker
- ___ @ $32.50 FL Allied Health

ILLINOIS EXAMS
- ___ @ $25.00 Chicago Police Officer
- ___ @ $25.00 Illinois Allied Health

The MIDWEST EXAMS
(Illinois, Indiana, Michigan, Minnesota, Ohio, and Wisconsin)
- ___ @ $30.00 Midwest Police Officer Exam
- ___ @ $30.00 Midwest Firefighter Exam

The SOUTH EXAMS
(Alabama, Arkansas, Georgia, Louisiana, Mississippi, North Carolina, South Carolina, and Virginia)
- ___ @ $25.00 The South Police Officer Exam
- ___ @ $25.00 The South Firefighter Exam

NATIONAL EDITIONS
- ___ @ $14.95 ASVAB (Armed Services Vocational Aptitude Battery)
- ___ @ $12.95 U.S. Postal Worker Exam
- ___ @ $15.00 Federal Clerical Worker Exam
- ___ @ $12.95 Bus Operator Exam
- ___ @ $12.95 Sanitation Worker Exam
- ___ @ $20.00 Allied Health Entrance Exams

NATIONAL CERTIFICATION EXAMS
- ___ @ $20.00 Home Health Aide Certification Exam
- ___ @ $20.00 Nursing Assistant Certification Exam
- ___ @ $20.00 EMT-Basic Certification Exam

CAREER STARTERS
- ___ @ $14.95 Computer Technician
- ___ @ $14.95 Health Care
- ___ @ $14.95 Paralegal
- ___ @ $14.95 Administrative Assistant/Secretary
- ___ @ $14.00 Civil Service

To Order, Call TOLL-FREE: **1-888-551-JOBS, Dept. A040**

Or, mail this order form with your check or money order* to:
LearningExpress, Dept. A040, 20 Academy Street, Norwalk, CT 06850

Please allow at least 2-4 weeks for delivery. Prices subject to change without notice. *NY, CT, & MD residents add appropriate sales tax

LearningExpress
An Affiliate Company of Random House, Inc.